GO

Everyday stories
of stopping to love

Claire Coggan

malcolm down

PUBLISHING

What others are saying . . .

'Some books I have to read. It's part of my job. But this book I was excited to read. I have known Claire for a number of years and have been so inspired by who she is and the gift that she carries. I couldn't wait to read this account of her journey and I was not disappointed. Her love for people, courage to follow Jesus and incredible anointing for healing is breathtaking and it seeps from every page of this book. I've had the joy of seeing Claire grow in her gifts and faithfully follow Jesus. I was inspired, provoked and led to worship as I read the stories and teaching that Claire so brilliantly unpacks in this book. If you want to get on adventure with God, Claire has pioneered a way for you to follow.'

Simon Holley, Senior Leader, King's Arms Church Bedford, UK and Catalyst Network, and author of *Sustainable Power; Creating a Healthy Culture of the Supernatural in the Church Today*

'My friend Claire has written an extraordinary account of what happens when you say yes to Jesus. Her stories of radical courage and humble obedience will inspire, provoke and encourage you to share the gospel with a fresh confidence, expectation and faith. Ultimately, this book will cause you to fall in love with Jesus, who laid His life down that ours might be lifted up. Read this book and imitate its message and may God use you powerfully to spread His love and power wherever you go.'

Phil Wilthew, Senior Leader at King's Arms Church, Bedford, UK and author of *Developing Prophetic Culture and Multiplying Disciples*

'In her book Claire beautifully and authentically shares her journey of learning how to introduce people to Jesus by expressing His love and His Kingdom to those she encounters on a daily basis, whether in a coffee shop, at work or in a supermarket. Through the many stories shared, Claire expresses a very different approach to evangelism simply by asking God, "Who do you want me to show your love to today?" The book is provoking, challenging and life changing for the reader, as it will tug at your heart a deeper desire to express greater compassion and God's presence to those you encounter daily.'

Karen Kircher, Director of Leading Leaders Ltd and author of *Called to Influence: How to Become a Kingdom-style Leader in Your Workplace*

'I am privileged to have Claire as a friend. I get to see first-hand her deep love for Jesus and her passion to make Him known to those not yet in relationship with Him. When we hang out she always has new stories to share of opportunities she's had to reveal Jesus to people, and many times I have watched her strike up a conversation with someone nearby in response to a prompt from the Holy Spirit. Claire lives what she has written, which means that each chapter is not just words on a page. Rather, this book carries with it an anointing to inspire faith and impart courage to all who read it. Jesus told His disciples to proclaim and demonstrate His Kingdom wherever they went. This is still His commission for every believer today. I want to whole-heartedly encourage you to read Claire's book. It will equip and empower you to say "yes" to God so that many who don't yet know Him encounter His love. It's time to rediscover the joy of the great commission. Will you go?'

Wendy Mann, International speaker based at King's Arms Church Bedford, UK and author of *Naturally Supernatural and Leading as Sons and Daughters*

'Far from the guilt- and performance-driven books on evangelism, Claire Coggan's book *Go: Everyday Stories of Stopping to Love* is a clear call for sons and daughters of God to join in His redeeming of this world. Filled with insightful wisdom and faith-filled testimonies, this book will ignite a fresh fire and activate you in a love-based evangelism that is not only changing the town Claire lives in, but it is changing the world. Claire makes it easy for our ordinary, everyday life to become charged with heaven's possibility! This book has unlocked in me again the wonder of salvation!'

Julian Adams, Director of Frequentsee and author of *Amplify: Refining Your Prophetic Gift and Kiss of the Father*

'Claire is the real deal. I've stood with her as we've prayed together in the street for people to be healed, I've followed her as she's responded to the Holy Spirit's leading and broken off from conversation to go and connect with a stranger, and I've watched her up close as she ministers with deep compassion to those in distress in coffee shops. She's a pioneer and an evangelist but, more than that, she's a woman who has been willing to surrender her day-to-day life to love others well. It's a privilege for me to call her my friend and I've no hesitation in wholeheartedly recommending this book. May it stir you for what's possible for someone willing to push past fear and see what adventures are on the other side.'

Steve Wilson, Evangelist and Senior Leader at King's Arms Church, Bedford, UK

Contents

Dedication

To my three amazing children:
Hannah, Sam and Pete.
Thank you for helping me to learn to be a mother
and for the love and grace you've shown me.
You are each such a precious gift.
My prayer is that you will always know
how deeply the Father loves you.

To my dear grandchildren:
Jude, Alfie, Eli, India, Nancy, Arnie, Sophie, Nelly and Luna.
You are each such a blessing.
May you shine so brightly that others see Jesus
in you and are drawn to their heavenly Father.

Acknowledgements

If someone had told me that one day I would write a book I probably wouldn't have believed them; I am not an academic or particularly clever with words. I take great encouragement from Paul, who said, *'For consider your calling, brothers: not many of you were wise according to worldly standards, not many were powerful, not many were of noble birth. But God chose what is foolish in the world to shame the wise; God chose what is weak in the world to shame the strong; God chose what is low and despised in the world, even things that are not, to bring to nothing things that are, so that no human being might boast in the presence of God'* (1 Corinthians 1:26-29).

There are so many people I want to thank. Alice, my first true friend, thank you for showing me unconditional love and introducing me to Jesus. I am forever grateful to you.

Thank you to many spiritual mothers and fathers. In my early days of walking with Jesus, I received richly through your teaching, your stories and your courage. Joy Dawson, I was so impacted by your passion to know and experience the love of God; and Rose Weiner, you imparted to me a love for God's word. Thank you to Floyd McClung, Ben Callander, Bill Davidson and many others for communicating the message of God's Father heart, and Tony Fitzgerald for both teaching and demonstrating the Kingdom. I still remember the nights at the hotel on Brighton seafront where we regularly saw many signs, wonders and miracles.

Writing this book would not have been possible without the encouragement of others and especially my darling husband. Tony, thank you for the way you celebrate me, for your patient encouragement, the endless cups of tea and for loving and serving me so selflessly. You truly are an example!'

Thank you Tracy, Julie and Carol and many others for your friendship and the journey we shared in Brighton. The steps of faith we took together and the stories will always stay with me, some of which are in this book.

Wendy, Jules, Karen and many other dear friends here in Bedford and further afield, thank you for cheering me on and for being excited for me to write this book. I'm so grateful for your encouragement. I'm so glad that we get to go on this journey together and I treasure your friendship.

Thank you to all of the TSM family for your encouragement, teaching and example. Just being around you ignites faith in me.

Thank you Tim, Martin, Steve, Libby and Jules for being such fun, faith-filled friends and courage buddies on our Costa adventure together.

Simon, Wendy and leaders at King's Arms Church, thank you for pioneering a culture where demonstrations of God's Kingdom are normal and to be expected.

Ali, I am so grateful to you! Without your superb editing skills this book would have only been half as good. Thank you for helping me to grow as a writer, to find my voice and for being excited for me to finish writing it.

Jules, thank you for your excellent design skills. I knew from the start I wanted you to design the cover.

Finally and most importantly I want to thank my heavenly Father. This book would not exist without these stories and these stories would not be possible without the incredible love, goodness and power of God. May every word and story bring glory to You, Jesus, and be multiplied through all who go and do likewise.

Introduction

We had just seen a lady touched by God. This lady had been in pain for six years as the result of an accident and she told us she needed carers to help her. After praying for her, all the pain had disappeared from her legs. The previous night she had been crying out and asking God, 'Where are you?' Now this lady wanted to scream and shout and tell everyone what God had done for her. As I told this story later to someone who doesn't yet know Jesus, he stared at me with his mouth open and then rubbing his arms he said, 'I don't know what to say, I've got goose bumps!'

Every day God wants to show people His perfect love and that He is not distant but kind, compassionate and forgiving. He wants to reveal to people that He is alive, that people can come to Him and know Him. The amazing thing is that He has chosen to use people like you and me to show and tell them.

I have a place where I like to sit each morning and spend time with the Father. One morning as I sat reading Psalm 78, I felt God speaking to me. It was one of those times, and I'm sure you've known them too, where God's words seemed to jump off the page as though they were freshly written for me to read in that moment.

Tell to the coming generation the glorious deeds of the LORD, and his might, and the wonders that he has done . . . teach to their children, that the next generation might know them, the children yet unborn, and arise and tell them to their children, so that they should set their hope in God and not forget the works of God.

I was so stirred and excited as I read these verses and I felt a fresh sense of urgency to tell and pass on stories of His goodness. Anyone who knows me will know that I am a storyteller; I love hearing and telling stories of what God is doing. One of my favourite things to do is to drink coffee with friends and talk about the things I've heard or seen God do. That morning as I meditated on these verses, wanting to respond, I felt God say to me, 'Keep boasting of My goodness, and keep telling others.' It was this encounter with God plus other words of prophetic encouragement that led me to write this book. This book of stories is my boast of His goodness.

The way Jesus taught about the Kingdom of God was to demonstrate and proclaim: 'show and tell'. As people heard Him teach about the Kingdom they also watched Him demonstrate it as He healed and delivered people. As they saw Him behave in a completely counter-cultural way it provoked them to ask questions, and as they encountered His love many followed Him. His disciples did the same and now we as His sons and daughters are His same message of love to the people we meet. We are His hands and feet in the places where we work, with our neighbours, in the supermarket or at the school gate.

Imagine being so convinced of His goodness and so filled with His love as we carry the treasure of this glorious gospel of Christ, that it overflows wherever we go and wherever we are. This is what I believe Jesus meant when He said, *'Go into all the world and proclaim the gospel'* (Mark 16:15). It was normal for the disciples and I believe it's meant to be normal for us too. So often we lack confidence, believing it is a ministry for the evangelists or those with a gift of healing and that God won't use us. The truth is if you are a disciple and friend of Jesus He wants to powerfully move through you. In Him you have everything you need to give to others. Jesus said, *'Freely you have received; freely give'* (Matthew 10:8 NIV).

Would you like to be more courageous in speaking to people about Jesus? Would you like to step out more in praying for the sick? Well Jesus wants this for you too. There are no 'Super Christians', no spiritually elite or special healers: you and I are they! As Jesus prepared to send out His disciples He said, *'As the Father has sent me, even so I am sending you'* (John 20:21).

There was a time when I would never have imagined praying in a public place for someone who I didn't know, and even if I'd had the courage, I'm not sure I would have expected much to happen. For me, praying for others was mostly done in safe areas like church meetings, small groups or at home. So much has changed! Over the last twelve years especially, as I've experienced a deeper revelation of God's love, it has led me to step out with greater boldness and faith. I remember the joy and surprise I felt the first time someone was healed when I prayed for them on the street, and someone's tearful response when I shared God's heart with them. Now when I sense the Holy Spirit leading me to someone I am often expectant that Jesus is about to do something wonderful!

Every day we meet people who when you ask them about God you discover that they have often only encountered religion and believe God is a distant being; many have not experienced the embrace of a loving Father. As Christ's ambassadors we get to represent the King of heaven here on earth, demonstrating His kindness, His mercy and love. As we listen, as we pray for healing and as we bring His words of hope, we have the honour of introducing people to Jesus. Nothing gives the Father more joy than watching us be Jesus in the flesh to the people He loves and died for; and it's not hard, it's simply loving people wherever we are. The Father is always at work and invites us to join Him. The following stories are mostly of ordinary everyday moments like these.

My prayer is that both other people's stories and my own will ignite faith and childlike courage in you to make Jesus known wherever you go. Let's be people who unashamedly boast of the goodness of God, expecting to see signs and wonders of His presence and telling others how great is His love. This love story is too good to keep to ourselves: we must pass it on!

Give ear, O my people, to my teaching;
incline your ears to the words of my mouth!
I will open my mouth in a parable;
I will utter dark sayings from of old,
things that we have heard and known,
that our fathers have told us.
We will not hide them from their children,
but tell to the coming generation
the glorious deeds of the LORD, and his might,
and the wonders that he has done.
He established a testimony in Jacob
and appointed a law in Israel,
which he commanded our fathers
to teach to their children,
that the next generation might know them,
the children yet unborn,
and arise and tell them to their children,
so that they should set their hope in God
and not forget the works of God.

Psalm 78:1-7

CHAPTER ONE

My Story

My frame was not hidden from you, when I was
being made in secret, intricately woven in the
depths of the earth. Your eyes saw my unformed
substance; in your book were written, every one
of them, the days that were formed for me,
when as yet there was none of them.

Psalm 139:15-16

Each one of us has a story to tell and pass on. Mine is of meeting Jesus and being transformed by the greatest love story of all time. I could never have imagined the days God had planned for me. At 16 I was a lost young girl living with shame and self-hatred desperately trying to find out who I was and looking for love. Only God can take someone so broken and make them whole. Steffany Gretzinger's song 'Out of Hiding' expresses it so well for me.

> *'Cause I loved you before you knew what was love*
> *I saw it all, still I chose the cross*
> *And you were the one that I was thinking of*
> *When I rose from the grave . . .*
> *And oh as you run, what hindered love*
> *Will only become part of the story?*[1]

I was adopted when I was just six weeks old. My parents weren't able to have children and chose first a boy called Stephen and then three years later they chose me. My mum and dad were hardworking people who believed in God in a nominal kind of way and who encouraged us to live moral lives. God was rarely mentioned in our house but at Christmas and Easter we went to church. I didn't like church much; it was a place of hard pews and hushed whispers and where you had to know to do the right thing at the right time. I remember Religious Education at primary school being very dull too; so dull I spent the time lacing and unlacing my shoes, willing it to be over.

What I do remember is being fascinated by clouds and thinking God might live somewhere beyond them. I also loved looking at pictures of angels in a prayer book with gold edges, and reading the prayers when I went to bed. Our parents occasionally quoted words of Jesus to us: *'Do to others as you would have them do to you'* and *'there is a narrow and a wide road'*. At the same time I remember my mum reading my palm and the tealeaves so, growing up, my experience of God and the spiritual world were very mixed.

There was quite a lot of tension and anxiety in our house. Our home was not a place where you could kick off your shoes or where it was ok to make mistakes; my mum had very high standards! My brother struggled with autism and I lied, stole and was insecure, and neither of us did well at school. For me, needing to feel accepted seemed to either push people away or get me into trouble. I know my parents loved me very much but I don't remember them ever telling me. My mum and dad came from a generation where words of encouragement and physical affection were often lacking. Working hard to give us the best education was their way of showing us love.

For a time I went to a Catholic school where we were taught the Bible and encouraged to confess our sins to a priest. The night before my first confessions I asked my mum what 'sins' were. I had been given a book with examples and she suggested I copied them all out onto a piece of paper. As I walked into the chapel the following day, clutching my sheet of paper, I saw a priest sat in a rocking chair at the side of the altar. He asked me to read aloud my sins and then, choosing one, he told me not to read other people's letters – something I'd copied out but which I knew I hadn't done. Of course it goes without saying I was probably guilty of most of the others on the list. Afraid of the 'holy silence' in the chapel, I didn't speak to the priest but after each time of confession, as I ran down the steps of the chapel, I hoped that God had somehow made me clean.

Despite my best efforts nothing really changed until I was about 14 when almost overnight I had a strong desire to be good. Tired of always feeling guilty I stopped stealing and I began to pray and read the Bible every night. It lasted several weeks but I couldn't keep it up: my new resolve was merely a religious exercise to try and feel better about myself. I remember even thinking about becoming a nun; it was nuns who ran our school and, despite later being expelled from there, something good was starting to rub off. I was beginning to search for God.

Around that time I read a small piece in the *Daily Telegraph* newspaper, which said, 'Do you want to know Jesus Christ?' Never having considered it before, I thought, 'Yes, I do!' There was an address at the bottom of the page and so I wrote off for more information. Suspecting my parents wouldn't approve I did it secretly and then I waited for the reply in the post, hoping they wouldn't ask me about it. The letter arrived with lots of information. I can't remember whether I wrote back or not but God was clearly awakening a desire in me to know Him.

I met Alice in my last year at secondary school. She had come to join our year whilst her parents were home from Tanzania where they had been working as missionaries. As she was a new girl to the class I saw it as an opportunity to make a friend. Despite my insecurities Alice was kind and accepting and over time we became the best of friends. Her mum, dad and five siblings showed me so much love that I quickly felt a part of their family and began to spend more time at their house than my own.

When Alice invited me to her church, I said yes. At first I felt very awkward. It was a church where all the women were conservatively dressed and wore headscarves and, as a hippy, I stood out. However, I kept going back because of their love. Without asking anything of me this wonderful group of people welcomed me, fed me, and loved me. I was experiencing what it was to belong even before I believed.

It was about a year later I began asking the question, 'What is it about these people and what do they have that I don't have?' I started properly listening to what was being preached every Sunday. I heard how God loved me and had sent Jesus to die in my place so that I could be forgiven of all my sin and have a new life in Him. There were stories regularly shared of people whose lives had been changed by encountering Jesus and I remember being impacted by the story a man told of seeing a vision of Jesus in his prison cell. Each time a story was shared I wanted to respond hoping the same would happen to me. A few people prayed with me to ask Jesus into my heart but because I couldn't feel anything I thought that Jesus must love other people but didn't actually love me.

My friend then started inviting me to rock concerts at a Baptist church nearby where Christian artists like Larry Norman[2] and Randy Stonehill[3] were playing. I loved their music and lyrics and every time I went I would end up crying and not know why. As I walked home from the concerts late at night I would talk to God, who I didn't yet know, hoping He might hear me. I had no idea then that God was actually pursuing me more than I was pursuing Him.

It happened a few weeks later. I was in the bathroom cleaning for my mum; I had a bottle of Vim in my hand and, thinking only about my pursuit of God, I slammed it down on the floor and said to God, 'Why won't you come into my life?' I went to bed that night feeling disappointed because again I felt nothing, but the following morning as I opened my eyes I was immediately aware of an incredible peace which flooded the whole of my body.

All my striving had gone and instead I felt joy; it just seemed to bubble up inside me. As I sat on my bed trying to make sense of what I was experiencing, a strange but wonderful thing happened. I felt a gentle breeze on my face, which I later came to understand was the Holy Spirit confirming His presence to me. Oh the joy! I wanted to tell the whole world that Jesus had come into my life. He had heard my cry.

Early days

It was 1973 and the time of the Jesus Movement[4] which had been sweeping across America and Europe since the late sixties. I had been a Christian for a week when I signed up to take part in a weeklong evangelistic event called Spree '73. Held between Earls Court and Wembley Stadium in London, it was a major Christian festival where Billy Graham spoke every evening to crowds of up to 30,000 people.

I went to London with no real idea what an evangelistic crusade was and feeling quite out of my depth. We spent the mornings attending seminars on subjects such as 'different religions' and 'discernment of spirits' and in the afternoons we were paired up and sent out into London either knocking on doors or talking to people in parks or on the streets about Jesus. We'd been given a small booklet called *The Four Spiritual Laws*[5] and we were encouraged to take people through it and, if they felt ready, to lead them in a prayer to receive Jesus. I don't think it occurred to me at the time whether I felt qualified to share the gospel with people. I was just a few days into reading *The Living Bible*[6] which I'd been given together with some *Daily Bread* notes.[7] I probably would have struggled to have entered into any kind of intelligent debate about the Christian faith or been able to have given a thorough explanation of the gospel. What I did know was that I'd met Jesus; I knew He loved me and I wanted to tell everyone that they could know Him too.

Each evening as we gathered at Wembley Stadium, stories were shared from the day followed by Billy Graham preaching the gospel and making an altar call, to which I responded most nights. Even though I had already received Jesus as Saviour and Lord, I wanted to be absolutely sure. Following Billy's powerful presentation of the gospel I felt compelled to get up out of my seat, along with hundreds of others, and go forward and kneel at the front. I can still remember a packed stadium singing, *Just as I am, without one plea but that Thy blood was shed for me. And that Thou bid'st me come to Thee O Lamb of God, I come.*[8]

The man on the train

I was on my way home from the festival very late one night when I met a man on the train. He'd nodded off and, thinking he might miss his stop, I nudged him and he woke up and began talking to me. It was 11.30 at night and the man was a bit drunk. In the moment I didn't think of the risk of talking to someone I didn't know at that time of night. I was just eager to tell him all about the festival and to share about Jesus with him. When we got off the train I was planning on heading straight home but the man wanted to continue talking. He started opening up to me about his broken marriage and his gambling addiction. I remember thinking I don't know how to help you or even what that looks like, I just know you need to meet Jesus. As he invited me into a dark and smoky bar on the station and offered to buy me a drink, I prayed a quick prayer asking God to please help me as I'd never been into a pub before. As we sat at a table his eyes began to fill with tears and I told him that if he'd like to follow me in a prayer he could know Jesus just like me. He bowed his head and prayed with me. I don't know what happened to him after that but as I left I told him of a church near to where he lived in Bristol where he could go and find out more. By the end of the week I remember it started to feel quite natural to ask the person next to me on a train or a bus whether they knew Jesus.

After this awesome training week, I hit some rocky ground. I returned to work and to church but I soon felt disillusioned; what I had just experienced wasn't happening in the church. I was emotionally up and down and I didn't know how to express the pain that was beginning to surface from my past or even that I needed to. Soon, without recognising it, I was slipping into a lifestyle of Christian 'dos and don'ts' where I felt happy when I did and guilty when I didn't! I was now trying to work for the love and acceptance I'd received by grace at the start. I compared myself with other Christians and I didn't think I measured up. When I read the Bible I knew I didn't measure up and, without community, it wasn't long before I started to give up!

I'd grown up in an environment where I'd had little space to make my own choices and decisions. I now wanted to be free of all restraints and the hippy lifestyle appealed to me. Hippies were young people looking for freedom, often through Eastern mysticism, harmony with nature, communal living and experimenting with a mix of art, music and drugs. I didn't get involved with Eastern mysticism or drugs or live-in community but I wanted to be free of convention and adopted this way of thinking. It seemed to offer a way of living and being that was liberating and so different from anything I had known. On the outside I behaved like a free spirit but inside I was actually far from free. It was all a mask. I was full of rejection with no sense of belonging or of my identity. Seeking escape from the reality of broken relationships there were many on the hippy trail like me who were simply running away.

I was working at the time at a residential special school and responsible for the care of six severely disabled young girls. I was young, naive and thrown in at the deep end into what was a very institutional way of living. These were days where disability was still shut away and where vulnerable children were sadly sometimes in the care of emotionally unhealthy adults. During my time there I encountered many things for the first time, including the occult. Despite trying to escape the controlling upbringing I had lived through, I soon found myself in a very unhealthy and controlling relationship. This relationship began to dominate me so much that I started to believe my life would never exist beyond it. One morning, feeling completely trapped, I picked up my Bible. As I opened it I read the story in Genesis where God told Abraham to leave his country, take all his family and belongings and go to a place that God would show him. Despite not really understanding it or feeling any real connection with God at the time, I believed He was speaking to me. Somehow I just knew to obey and immediately handed my notice in and left. It was as though God was airlifting me out.

With nowhere to go I moved to London and for a short time took a job as a nanny before moving on to work in a children's home in Guildford. I'd stopped going to church and the next few years were a turbulent time as I was trying to make sense of who I was and wrestling with a need for love. Instead of finding it in God, I began looking for it in relationships. I had also decided to try and search for my birth mother but I soon discovered the law didn't allow me access to my birth records without my parents' permission, something I knew I couldn't ask them for. Feeling let down I became depressed, I had suicidal thoughts and I began drinking heavily to try and squash the pain and disappointment I was feeling. Months later, after an unsuccessful court appeal, I reluctantly put the search behind me and tried to move on.

By now I had drifted far from God and I felt I could no longer call myself a Christian. I had been dating a young man for some time who was on his own spiritual journey of Eastern philosophy and transcendental meditation and he began to express his desire to marry me. As he began speaking about our future together I suddenly found myself saying to him, 'I'm sorry, but I can't marry you because you are not a Christian.' I didn't know in that moment where these words had come from and I don't know who was more shocked. The oddest thing was that I didn't feel any great disappointment about ending our relationship. This was a pivotal moment where God woke me up and showed me this wasn't His plan for me and, like the Prodigal,[9] I came to my senses. As I turned around, God seemed to point me in the right direction. I had a new desire to follow Him and a passion to tell others about Jesus.

Fresh zeal

In this new season of my life, everywhere I went it seemed there were fresh opportunities to share the gospel. I was 22 and training to be a qualified houseparent of children with cerebral palsy at a college near Oxford. There were just 15 of us on the course and I was full of faith for the other students to come to know Jesus. I befriended a girl who was already a Christian. We decided each day to get up very early and, taking a boat out on the river which ran alongside the college, we'd pray for the other students. I'm not sure why we didn't just meet in each other's room to pray as neither of us could row a boat to save our lives and it caused much amusement to the houseboat owners as our little boat kept circling the river each morning. In the college coffee bar where we all hung out and socialised my friend and I regularly sang songs about Jesus and had animated conversations about God into the small hours of the morning. It was an exciting time and it wasn't long before three students gave their lives to Jesus. Whenever we saw any sign of hunger to know Him we would rush off between lectures to the bathroom to pray for them.

As part of our course we were encouraged to volunteer in the community and my friend and I chose to help at the nearby psychiatric hospital. I chose this hoping to overcome a fear I'd had since visiting an aunt in a similar hospital as a child. Over the weeks we befriended a man there, cutting his hair and taking him out on trips. Around this time I saw that a local Baptist church was holding an evangelistic meeting and had invited a 'Painter Preacher'. Not exactly sure what that was I decided anyhow it was a great opportunity to invite as many of our students as possible, including our friend from the hospital. After borrowing the college minibus and rounding everyone up, twelve of us walked in a little late to discover the only spare seats were on the front row. It wasn't long before I realised the painting was going to be given to the person who had invited the most people to the service. I remember, with embarrassment, not wanting to look at my friends for fear they'd think I'd invited them under false pretences. After a gospel appeal and several responses, we were duly given the painting. I have often wondered why this unusual approach to evangelism? I guess this man simply wanted to use his talent as an artist to reach people with the gospel.

Those who had become Christians were now becoming hungry to know more and one evening asked if I'd lead a Bible study in my room. I really didn't know how and I felt panicky inside as they all gathered around my bed and then looked at me. I remember just choosing a passage at random and reading it out. It was about forgiving one another. What happened next could only have been a Holy Spirit encounter. As we stood in a circle with our arms around each other and prayed, one by one we asked each other for forgiveness even to the very motives of our hearts. There were tears of repentance and at the end we looked at the clock and realised we had been standing together for well over an hour without realising it. We were all deeply affected by the experience. In my weakness I had been completely dependent on God with no idea of the outcome, and I learned from this that often more happens when we don't know what we're doing than when we do.

Hunger for the Holy Spirit

The Christian coffee house circuit was a popular setting for outreach ministry at that time and after leaving college I occasionally played and sang in coffee bars, pubs or with friends.

One time I was visiting one of my friends in Lancaster. Emmy had come to know Jesus at college and she and I had the opportunity to sing and share the gospel in a café that was next door to a Christian bookshop. We both noticed a young girl had responded to our invitation to know Jesus and so I took her out to the back of the bookshop to pray with her. I remember feeling so excited that she had responded but at the same time anxious about whether I was saying the right words as I led her in a prayer to receive Jesus.

I had been baptised in water but had not yet encountered the Holy Spirit. Baptism in the Spirit wasn't really mentioned in the church I went to and when I enquired I was told to speak privately to a church elder in his home. Even though I did, I came away from the meeting more confused and with a sense that I shouldn't worry about it anymore. It was four years later that some friends and I went away to seek God together. We headed for the Lake District and spent time reading scripture and praying. We all became convinced that baptism in the Spirit was a promise to us from the Father and, on my return, wherever there was an opportunity, I looked to receive this gift. After many times of receiving prayer and still not speaking in tongues, I began to believe that maybe it was a gift given just to some – something that was sometimes taught back then.

One day I was in a meeting where I heard a lady bring a beautiful song in tongues and it touched me deeply. I went to her to encourage her, explaining in a matter of fact way that I didn't have the gift of tongues myself. She seemed concerned and took the opportunity to pray for me. Still nothing changed, until a year later one of our church leaders prayed for me and coached me through the battle I was having between my mind and my mouth! I faithfully spoke the three words God gave me for a very long time. Then one day, after hearing a man preach on the greatness of God, something broke and a river of tongues flowed out of me.

A time of reaping

As the church was being awakened in the things of the Spirit, there was a wealth of Christian singer-songwriters emerging who were taking risks and inspiring a young generation with 'Jesus Music'. People like Larry Norman, Randy Stonehill, Phil Keaggy,[10] Malcolm and Alwyn,[11] Keith Green[12] and many more. I loved their music and spent many evenings playing their songs to friends hoping the words would inspire them to follow Jesus.

Since qualifying as a houseparent I was now working at a special school in West Sussex, which was pioneering a teaching approach for children with cerebral palsy. It was an exciting opportunity and I loved the children and worked with a great team. The school attracted a lot of international visitors for short-term placements who came to see what we were doing. Living on the job meant we got to know each other well and God gave me many natural opportunities to share Jesus with people who visited while I was there.

One night my friends had gone out for the evening and invited me to go with them but I stayed back. God must have planned it because well into the night I got talking to a girl who had recently arrived on placement and who told me she was a Quaker.[13] Having not before come across anyone who was a Quaker, I asked her what it meant to her and soon realised she wasn't that sure either. As I told her what being a Christian meant to me, she warmed to my passion about knowing God personally and, by the end of the night, I knew without any doubt that she was going to soon give her life to Jesus; God had given me a gift of faith. I told my friends and we all prayed for her that week. The following Sunday she came to church, and that's when she gave her life to Jesus.

A few months later I had another opportunity to introduce a friend to Jesus. I was sharing a flat with a girl called Katy who said she was a Catholic. Whenever we spoke about our beliefs we seemed to end up arguing and disagreeing, which didn't feel right. As I was wrestling with this I felt God say to stop discussing beliefs and to invite her to church, and I was really surprised when Katy agreed to come. After a couple of weeks I discovered that for the first time she was enjoying being part of a community of people who loved each other and who had fun together. She said she had not experienced this in the Catholic churches she had previously been to and she continued coming. One Sunday shortly after this she went forward to give her life to Jesus.

Eventually I moved away and lost touch with Katy but, thirty-four years later, I received a letter. She told me she'd had a dream about me and remembering my faith in Jesus asked if I would go and visit her. It was hard to see how much Katy had suffered physically, losing her sight and now in a wheelchair due to multiple sclerosis. Before leaving I prayed that God would heal her and I encouraged her to keep believing and trusting in Jesus.

Meeting Tony

One last and important story from these early days! In 1979 I met my husband Tony. He was serving in a pizza restaurant that Youth with a Mission[14] were running whilst also touring with a dance drama called *Toymaker & Son*.[15] Excited by the ways YWAM were reaching out with the gospel, I was soon following Tony and the team as they toured schools, churches and shopping centres, taking friends along with me to watch. I regularly attended meetings YWAM were running including a 'Disciples for Jesus' course. Initially the gospel was the main attraction but soon it became Tony as well and, in the September of 1980, Tony and I were married. With little money between us we started our married life in a small caravan, which Tony owned, that was in the grounds of the YWAM base. It was soon after this, as a result of an outreach into the town, that a church was planted in Crawley which we both became part of. This was the first of many churches which grew into a large family of churches called Church of the Nations.[16]

At weekends I used to help Tony serve in the pizza restaurant and during that time we began to notice a couple called James and Bethany who regularly came in on a Saturday night. As we got chatting a friendship began to grow between us. A few weeks later Bethany told us how, just that week, she had been standing at her sink looking out of the window and feeling as though something was missing in her life. She was happily married with a beautiful little girl but she said she knew there had to be more. At the same time Jehovah Witnesses were visiting her but they couldn't always answer her questions. She commented how serious they were but how our passion for Jesus drew her. A couple of visiting speakers were at our church the following weekend and we decided to invite our friends along. It was soon afterwards that Bethany, and then later her husband James, gave their lives to Jesus.

Looking back I remember these early days of following Jesus as such fruitful times where often we got to reap where others had sown. In John 4:37-38 we read that Jesus said, *'One sows and another reaps. I sent you to reap that for which you did not labour. Others have laboured, and you have entered into their labour.'* I believe in heaven we will be so surprised as we get to see the fruit of where we, and others, have faithfully sown the seeds of the gospel through our words, our actions and our prayers.

Since those earliest days, I am so thankful for all God has shown me and taught me. I probably wouldn't now encourage a young girl on her own to go into a bar late at night to share the gospel. However, one thing I am certain of: I don't ever want to stop sharing the message that is 'simply Jesus'. I don't want to trade the raw passion of encountering Him for a relationship without risk or adventure. Jesus said in Matthew 10:39, *'If you cling to your life, you will lose it; but if you give up your life for me, you will find it'* (NLT). The writer to the Hebrews also reminds us not to throw away our confidence, which has a great reward, but to live by faith and not shrink back. I wonder how many of us were bolder sharing the gospel when we first met Jesus than we are now? I hope through this book to help us discover or rediscover courage to speak about Jesus wherever we are; a boldness to love others that can only come as we first know how loved we are.

CHAPTER TWO

The Greatest Love Story

Greater love has no one than this,
that someone lay down his life for his friends.

John 15:13

Do you remember when you first encountered Jesus? Do you remember the excitement and joy as you told others? I didn't have many words to explain it but I knew that something had changed on the inside and I would never be the same.

Our confession of faith in Jesus can be met by all kinds of responses. I remember trying to explain to my dad who wasn't a Christian. He saw it as something I was into and just another phase, and there had been many! I remember crying with frustration because he didn't understand, yet I knew that Jesus had come to live inside of me. Romans 8:16 says, *'The Spirit himself bears witness with our spirit that we are children of God.'* My message of Jesus and His love had come out of an encounter with Him.

When we meet Jesus we don't encounter a set of religious beliefs but, like the woman at the well, we meet the Living One. When we open our heart to receive Him everything changes. The Samaritan woman said, *'Come, see a man who told me all that I ever did'* (John 4:29). As a result of her encounter with Jesus a whole town came out to meet Him and many chose to follow Him.

Every believer has a story of how they met Jesus. Maybe, like me, it was through a friend or maybe a parent or sibling. Perhaps someone spoke to you on the street or maybe a colleague at work invited you to an Alpha Course.[1] Almost everyone hears the gospel from someone else; this is often God's way of communicating the good news. When Andrew met Jesus he quickly went and told Simon his brother and it was Philip who introduced Nathaniel to Jesus. I often ask people, 'Do you know Jesus and have you met Him?' And sometimes I share my story. The story of every believer is unique and a powerful demonstration of God's amazing grace and points people to Him. In the midst of someone wanting to debate I have often seen their expression change as I have shared my personal story with them. I saw this one time when some friends and I were in our town.

We met a young man called Liam. As we got into conversation Liam told us he was an atheist. My friend asked him if he'd ever thought about why he was an atheist, which I thought was a great question. Liam's reply was that he didn't know if God was real because he had never experienced Him. We told Liam that he could and encouraged him to ask God to reveal Himself to him. At the same time I felt the Holy Spirit prompt me to tell him some of my story and how I had encountered the presence of Jesus in my bedroom. Liam began to well up saying he felt embarrassed crying in the street but that he had never heard anything like it before. We saw his heart soften and, after sharing the gospel with him, Liam said he wanted to receive Jesus for himself, and there and then he did. What is poignant about this story is that very day Liam had just come from his father's funeral. At a very vulnerable time in his life he encountered His heavenly Father! We felt such joy, I remember wanting to dance in the street! We kept in touch with Liam and some months later he was baptised and is now connected with a local church in our town.

Overcoming fear with love

I am convinced that the greatest gift we can ever give someone is to introduce them to Jesus! The gospel is the greatest love story and it is such good news! Even though we know this is true it takes boldness and courage to step out and share it with others. We not only have to face our own fears but also the fact that there is a very real resistance to truth. Paul himself prayed that God would give him courage to speak. He said, *'[Pray] also for me, that words may be given to me in opening my mouth boldly to proclaim the mystery of the gospel'* (Ephesians 6:19).

Fear is probably the biggest enemy we face when we think about talking to people about Jesus or offering to pray for them. It feels awkward approaching people. Maybe we're not sure what to say, how to start the conversation and, if we do offer to pray, fearful that nothing will happen. On the journey God has taken me on I have become convinced that although speaking to people about Jesus always takes an act of courage on our part, when it comes from a place of love and compassion it becomes our great joy.

Ten years ago God began to show me this in a fresh way whilst attending a training course in Bedford, called 'Training in Supernatural Ministry'.[2] On this course, as I got free from some things that were holding me back, God re-awakened in me a passion to tell others about Jesus; the same passion I had known early on in my Christian life. I began to see how I'd become very busy serving God in the church and where telling others about Jesus had started to become more about numbers and ticking boxes than a passion for His Kingdom that I'd first known. What changed was God showing me afresh His love for me, and how I was His daughter first before I did anything for Him. As this revelation of His love and my identity started to move from my head to my heart I became much more free: free from performance and working for God's approval. This is an ongoing journey for me and maybe for many of us but I've come to see this is key to us living the supernatural life Jesus has called us to live out.

When we know how much God loves us and are secure in our identity, sharing Jesus isn't a pressure; it becomes a natural overflow of His life in us.

When Jesus asked His disciples the question 'Who do you say I am?' He was asking them an identity question. Peter replied, '"You are the Christ, the Son of the Living God." And Jesus answered, ". . . Flesh and blood has not revealed this to you, but my Father who is in heaven"' (Matthew 16:16-17). Jesus was teaching through this the importance of our need for revelation of both His identity and of ours in Him. This was huge and it was what the early church was founded on. This revelation enabled Peter to do the things he did, even to walk on water. When we know we are first and foremost a son or daughter of God, sharing the good news of the Kingdom becomes something of great joy because it is what we are made for. This is part of our identity.

Even though the disciples knew great joy I am sure they, too, sometimes encountered fear. Like them we are all on a journey of learning to live like Jesus. I remember the first time I tried to speak to a stranger on the street and how nervous I felt, how my words were all jumbled. I also remember once being in a café and offering to pray for a lady who opened up to me about her life and her sore hand. I was so nervous after praying I didn't even ask her how her hand was, and it was I who changed the subject! Fear of rejection and of nothing happening overwhelmed me. I still get a bit nervous when I step out and speak to a stranger about Jesus but as I've grown in understanding that my identity is not wrapped up in my performance, I have become free to love people knowing the outcome is always up to God.

I don't know what your experiences of evangelism have been like. Even the word 'evangelism' can sometimes be unhelpful. It can bring up images for us of awkward and uneasy conversations that we've had or styles of street preaching that have made us cringe. I've started to see how evangelism isn't meant to be something we slip out of church and 'do' but a lifestyle of loving the people God puts in front of us each day. Showing people how much God loves them reveals His Kingdom and as they experience His Kingdom it prepares them to meet the King. All of us are called to speak about Jesus and to demonstrate who He is and I hope through my journey and stories to encourage and equip you in doing just that. Every day we get to carry the most joy-filled message of good news, telling people how much the Father loves them.

Let's remind ourselves of the gospel

When Jesus came to earth He came to reveal the Father. He said, *'I and the Father are one'* (John 10:30), *'I have come down from heaven, not to do my own will but the will of him who sent me'* (John 6:38). God who is love sent His message of love to us in the person of Jesus. Jesus came to show us what the Father is like and to lead us to Him. This beautiful gospel is the Father's invitation to us to come home and it never changes.

The gospel

When we look at the gospel we can see why it is such good news. God is good! His goodness flows eternally and unceasingly; it is who He is. The Bible tells us that in the beginning everything God created was very good and He took pleasure over all He had made. When God created us He made us to be just like Him and to enjoy an unhindered relationship with Him. We see this in Genesis. He provided everything Adam and Eve needed. Everything was perfect in the garden, even the temperature! There was nothing to distract them from knowing God and enjoying one another.

Satan, once chief amongst angels and described as the morning star, had himself known God's goodness. Now banished from heaven because of seeking his own autonomy and glory, he was persuading Adam and Eve to do exactly the same. God had said to Adam and Eve they could enjoy the fruits of any of the trees in the garden but not to eat of the tree of life. By suggesting God was withholding something good from them Satan tempted them to disobey God's command. Adam and Eve exchanged what they knew of God's goodness for a lie, which led them to sin. As a result of their sin they became separated from God and, as a result, we did too.

The good news, though, is that God never wanted there to be any separation between Him and us. It was always His plan that we would be His sons and daughters walking in relationship with Him. It's incredible that the God of all creation, who is holy and dwells in unapproachable light, planned for us to know Him without anything separating us from Him. This is why God sent Jesus, fully God becoming fully man to restore what was broken. The greatest transaction in the history of the universe was Jesus laying down His life for us, taking our sin upon Himself and dying in our place. Through the death and resurrection of Jesus our sin has been completely cancelled and we have been raised with Him to newness of life. As Paul tells us, not only are we now forgiven but we have been adopted as sons and daughters. We have become reinstated as heirs and coheirs with Christ, called to rule and reign with Him. When we receive this immense and undeserved gift of grace and put our trust in Jesus we are forever restored. Imagine, the God of all creation who is pure and holy invites us near and promises that He will draw near to us!

The truth is we are all made for this relationship; our spirit cries out to know God and to be known by Him. In different stages of my life I know I have often been a bit like the younger or older brother we read about in Luke 15: sometimes running away and sometimes proud and self-reliant. I've come to see that we are all living like orphans pursuing meaning and significance in the wrong places until we discover the Father's love for us and come home to Him. This gospel of grace is the greatest love story and we must not keep it to ourselves. We bring the Father such joy when we go and tell people about Him because God's heart is always to bring restoration: that's what Jesus died for! Jesus really is the hope of the world and people are waiting to encounter Him.

If Jesus was walking on the earth today I imagine He would be walking through our towns and cities being moved with compassion for the lonely, the broken and those who are hurting. Perhaps He would be walking by the river or hanging out in cafés and bars. Wherever He would be, we know He would be amongst people. And now He has sent us. John writes in 1 John 4:17. 'As he is so also are we in this world.' We are His hands and feet. We are His message of love. Nothing gives the Father more joy than watching us be like Jesus in the flesh to the people He loves and died for. I remember one time I was going up the stairs in a shop and a lady said, 'You go in front of me because I have to walk slowly with my bad back.' I stopped and asked her about her back and got to pray for her there on the stairs as people filed past her, and when she walked to the top she said all the pain had gone away. She got to encounter the God who loves her and who knew she was in pain.

Paul describes us as ambassadors of Christ. Just like an ambassador is sent as a representative of his government in another country, as ambassadors of Christ we too are sent. We have been sent to represent the King and His Kingdom.

We are each a living message of God's great love, His supernatural love that saves, heals and sets people free, and He has chosen to reveal Himself through you and me!

I wonder when you hear this if it fills you with excitement or with fear?

As you'll soon see, this book isn't about formulas or methods of how to do evangelism; it's mostly a book of stories. Stories of when others and I have said yes to God and of how, supernaturally, God has led us to the people He wanted us to meet. For me these have mostly been just in my everyday life. This is prophetic evangelism and I believe it is the life Jesus and the disciples modelled for us.

CHAPTER THREE

Called to Shine

Let your light shine before others, so that
they may see your good works and give
glory to your Father who is in heaven.

Matthew 5:16

As we read the gospels we see that wherever Jesus went He proclaimed the good news of the Kingdom and demonstrated it with signs, wonders and miracles, inviting people to follow Him. When Jesus called Peter and Andrew, He said, 'Follow me, and I will make you fishers of men' (Matthew 4:19). In this one statement Jesus was showing them what it meant to be His disciple: disciples who go and make disciples. What encourages me is that even though they knew He had chosen and called them and that they were His friends, they still had some growing to do. Just like us, they still had to learn His ways and understand their identity. As they spent time with Jesus they saw Him face every situation imaginable. They saw His humility, authority and compassion. They saw Him laugh, they saw Him get angry and they saw Him cry. They witnessed the priority of His relationship with His Father and they learned to pray. Jesus was their teacher, mentor and friend. He taught them, He trusted them, He rebuked them, He comforted them, He showed them that He would never leave them and He restored them when they abandoned Him. He never failed them: Jesus discipled them!

When Jesus sent the disciples out He gave them authority to heal the sick, to cast out demons and to raise the dead and that's what they went and did! He said to them, 'Freely you have received; freely give' (Matthew 10:8 NIV). It's often struck me that Jesus didn't give them any methods, formulas or tracts. He simply told them where to go, what they didn't need to take, to be aware of persecution and not to be afraid. Jesus had both prepared them and trusted them to go and do the same things He was doing.

I wonder if you ever asked yourself the question 'What is my ministry?' I used to, and especially when I saw people doing great things for God. I knew I loved God but I worried that I might have missed His purpose for me. What I now know is that my ministry is to be His daughter and as His daughter He has called me to shine brightly wherever I am. God has spoken to me several times and told me He has called me to introduce people to Jesus.

Whether you would see yourself as an evangelist or not I believe you are called to shine wherever God has placed you. Whether it's next to the person in your office or school, the people you do business with or those you interact with as you travel to work. Maybe it's around the people you meet as you do your shopping, go to have your hair cut or walk your dog.

Being an earthly representative of Jesus is our full-time ministry.

'For what we proclaim is not ourselves, but Jesus Christ as Lord . . . For God, who said, "Let light shine out of darkness," has shone in our hearts to give the light of the knowledge of the glory of God in the face of Jesus Christ. But we have this treasure in jars of clay, to show that the surpassing power belongs to God and not to us' (2 Corinthians 4:5-7).

Some years ago I started having dreams where I was sharing about Jesus with people and praying for the sick in shops and supermarkets and, soon after, this actually started to happen. It began with me starting to notice people. I remember one day sitting in a café and feeling love for a complete stranger sat at a nearby table and I knew I had never felt this before. Sometimes when I was just walking along the street, sitting on a train or standing in a supermarket queue, I just felt drawn to share God's love with people. To put this in some context, during the previous six months of the training course I was attending, I'd taken part in weekly outreach on the streets of Bedford. Through prophetic words, simple acts of kindness or through physical healing, we had seen people encounter God's love in so many wonderful ways. I remember on just one afternoon how two people received Christ, a man's hip was healed after saying he didn't believe in healing and another man who, after being healed of a football injury, said he was going home to give his life to Jesus, which he did. I remember, too, that on the same afternoon a man who'd had a negative experience of religion and of church opened up to us, saying no one had ever told him how to hear God before. As a result of sharing God's love with him he took up the challenge to go home and read the gospel of John and talk to God, asking Him to reveal Himself!

At the time I was living on the south coast and eager to see God do the same in my hometown. I began to pray and then, going out, I would ask God, 'Who do you want me to show your love to today?' Almost immediately opportunities started opening up. The first time it happened, I had just asked God this very question when a man in the street drew level with me and said, 'Can you help me, please?' I remember thinking this must be God! The man was anxious and unsteady on his feet and explained that he suffered with Parkinson's disease. He asked if I'd help him get a taxi. I took his arm and, helping him along, I found him a seat whilst I called a taxi and then helped him into it. I remember thinking afterwards, what if God had wanted me to offer to pray for his healing? – even though, at the time, that would have taken a big step of faith on my part. As I was berating myself for not having asked him, I heard the Father say to me, 'You asked Me who you could show My love to, and that's what you did; you showed him kindness.'

Jesus showed kindness to people in so many ways through His acceptance and through the way He spoke to them, as well as by healing and setting people free. Jesus' kindness was and is so extravagant. I began to notice that the more I asked God who I could show His love to and the more available I made myself, the more He kept arranging opportunities. Sometimes in coffee shops, in the supermarket queue, in the hairdresser's or at the bus stop, God was calling me outside of the church building. I knew God was telling me, 'This is where I've called you to shine.'

When we read the gospels we see Jesus didn't invite people to the temple to hear Him but mostly He walked amongst people and spoke to them. I love what Bob Johnson writes in his book *Love Stains*:

Imagine God using you just the way you are to touch the people in your everyday life. A simple smile, a gentle word of encouragement, a prophetic statement, a gift given at just the right time, courage to hold the heartbroken, ability to love the unlovable, to heal the sick all because Jesus is in you. Just by being you.

Imagine Jesus being in the supermarket, in the hairdresser's or at the school gate. Imagine Jesus being in the doctor's waiting room, in the hospital or your office. Imagine being Jesus to your family.[1]

Jesus in the coffee shop

I first met Sophia when I invited her to join my table in a café, as there were no other spaces for her to sit. It seemed easy to engage in conversation and even though her English was limited we were soon sharing with one another about our lives, our families, and our beliefs. Sophia was from Iran and had been brought up a Muslim. After fleeing an abusive marriage she was now married to an Iranian man in the UK who was good and kind to her. Having had to leave her grown up children in Iran she clearly missed them and worried about them. Over coffee, as I listened and showed love to her, she asked me lots of questions about my experience of knowing Jesus. When she had to leave, Sophia told me she would like to meet up for coffee again and gave me her phone number, even inviting me to her house. We continued to meet regularly and she would often ask me what I believed about marriage, divorce, money, prayer and family.

One time when we were together, Sophia told me she sometimes prayed three times a day facing Mecca and said it gave her some peace of mind. In the same conversation she said that when she read the Quran it told her of the laws she had broken and the torture that she deserved. I could see how fearful she was. Using a combination of serviettes and placemats I explained the gospel to her. How God loved her so much that Jesus had taken on Himself the punishment she deserved so that she could know peace and a relationship with Him as her Father forever. I was so happy when Sophia asked me if I'd write the gospel out simply for her in her notebook and if I could get her a Bible in Farsi!

Over weeks and months our friendship grew and when we weren't meeting in the coffee shop we would meet at her home where she regularly treated me to a lavish feast of Middle-Eastern hospitality. One time she let me pray for her and Jesus took pain away from her leg. We met as couples a few times and after once coming to church, Sophia did part of our Alpha Course. Sophia struggles to accept Jesus is God and told me how afraid she would be to convert from Islam to Christianity; as far as I know she still hasn't opened her heart to Jesus. What I do know is that Sophia has both heard and experienced the good news of the gospel many times and I got to introduce her to Jesus, which is what He asked me to do.

Jesus in the supermarket

Sometimes we may only have a small window of opportunity to share the love of Jesus with people. I was at the till in the supermarket when the lady on the checkout started telling me she had shoulder pain. I knew the Holy Spirit was getting my attention and so I asked her if she'd like me to pray for her. She smiled and said, 'Yes please!' Leaning across I prayed a short prayer commanding all the pain to leave and then asked her how it was. She looked surprised and said, 'It's a lot better, and your hand was hot too.' I asked her if it was completely better and she said, 'Yes, apart from a little bit of stiffness.' After praying once more and commanding all the stiffness to go she told me it was better and then asked if I had some kind of healing power. I told her that it was Jesus who had taken away her pain because He loved her. Her colleague then came across and the lady told her that I had just done healing on her shoulder and her colleague replied, 'Yes, I saw it!' I told them both again that it was Jesus and how He loved them. The next customer came through so I had to quickly pack my shopping and say goodbye. As I left, the lady kept thanking me.

Jesus at the bus stop

It was a brief encounter between stops. I was standing in the queue waiting to get on a bus when I suddenly became aware of a lady staring at me. In fact it was more than a stare; it was as though she was looking right into me. Sensing the Holy Spirit, I asked her if she was ok. She told me she was unwell and so, as we got on the bus, I made sure she had a seat and prayed that I might get to sit next to her. The bus was busy but I did get to sit with her and I asked her what was going on. She told me she had been having some tests but not had the results and was clearly very anxious. I asked her if I could pray for her and, smiling, she told me she knew some people like me and was glad for me to pray for her. She then had to get off at the next stop.

If you could never imagine having courage to speak to strangers like this, never mind pray for them, I understand. I used to feel exactly the same. I still have to step through fear every time I say, 'Excuse me . . .'! Fear of what people will think, fear of getting it wrong or of nothing happening when we pray can paralyse us. It's love that sets us free. Being secure in who God says we are and being overcome with His love for the person in front of us enables us to step through fear. Love for people always attracts the Holy Spirit and He has encounters just waiting for us to step into where all kinds of good things will happen.

We are the light of the world

Jesus said to His disciples, *'As long as I am in the world, I am the light of the world'* (John 9:5), then knowing He was soon to be leaving the earth He said to His disciples and to us, *'You are the light of the world.'*

> **Jesus didn't say you are the light of the church,
> He said you are the light of the world.**

I think Jesus must have known our tendency to get distracted or to be afraid because He exhorted us not to hide our light or like salt to lose our saltiness. He said, *'A city set on a hill cannot be hidden. Nor do people light a lamp and put it under a basket, but on a stand, and it gives light to all in the house. In the same way, let your light shine before others, so that they may see your good works and give glory to your Father who is in heaven'* (Matthew 5:14-16).

We may think the words of the song 'This little light of mine, I'm going to let it shine'[2] are simplistic but there is a timeless truth they convey. They remind us we are not just to shine around one another in the church. We must not simply bunker down, living out our lives for Jesus the best we can until we die and go to be with Him. Instead we are called to be a brightly shining light wherever we go. Psalm 50:2 says, *'Out of Zion, the perfection of beauty, God shines forth.'* We, the church, are called to arise, shine and reflect the light and glory of Jesus.

We are light carriers and glory carriers pointing people to Jesus.

We are called to demonstrate His nature through our acts of service, preferring others, showing honour and being trustworthy. We are called to glorify Jesus through our speech and conduct, being slow to anger and quick to listen and by choosing to live out our lives not simply to please men but to please God. Jesus described John the Baptist as a burning and shining light that people followed. I believe our lives are meant to provoke people to ask, 'Who are you and what is it about you that is different?' The more we are full of God and full of the joy of knowing Him the brighter we'll shine wherever we are!

Jesus said, *'You did not choose me, but I chose you and appointed you that you should go and bear fruit and that your fruit should abide.'* It was always God's idea that we would be fruitful. Jesus tells us in John 15 that abiding in Him and staying close is the key to our fruitfulness.

One night a few years ago, God spoke to me about this in a dream. I heard God say very clearly, 'Stay close to Me and be fully you wherever you are.' There have been a few times where God has spoken through sentences or phrases in my dreams to get my attention and as I lay there I realised that God was speaking to me about intimacy and identity. The next day as I was looking out of our lounge window I noticed two very tall sunflowers which were fully out in a garden opposite. I hadn't noticed them before and I was struck in that moment how audacious sunflowers are, so much taller than other plants and when fully out they draw people to notice them; there is nothing hidden about a sunflower. As I was looking at these flowers and thinking this, I heard the Father speak three words – 'bold', 'beautiful', 'brave' – and He said to me, 'And that's who I've made you to be.' I immediately felt such deep affirmation from the Father and was reminded of Psalm 34:5, *'Those who look to him are radiant, and their faces shall never be ashamed.'* Shame is something I have struggled a lot with through my life. Shame says we are not enough and it causes us to hide. It robs us of our voice, so we become silent and hide behind other people's voices. It is shame that stops us being all God has made us to be, but shame is not our portion because Jesus took it for us at the cross. The astounding truth is that God actually wants to show us off so that as others look at us they will see Him. I love what Mike Pilavachi says: 'The greatest evangelistic tool we have? Disciples. Men and women who look, sound and smell like Jesus.'

Do you know and believe that as a son or daughter you are anointed with the same anointing as Jesus? His Holy Spirit is in you. We are light bringers in dark places, we get to shift atmospheres because of the peace and hope we carry. This is our identity. Our identity is who God says we are. It is Christ in us, the hope of glory. Only God can reveal Himself to people so that they open their hearts to Him, but through us, as His ambassadors, He makes His appeal. As we go where people are and listen and follow the Holy Spirit, we point people to Him and they can experience His extravagant love.

One day I was waiting to try clothes on in a shop (you could say minding my own business), when all of a sudden the lady managing the changing rooms said to me, 'I fell down the stairs last night; I don't think I should have come into work today, I am in so much pain.' After telling her that I am a Christian and that I know Jesus loves to heal people, I asked her if I could pray for Jesus to take the pain away. She looked surprised but then said, 'That's generous of you.' I remember thinking in that moment how generously God wanted to show her His love. Asking if it was ok to lay my hand on her back, I prayed a short prayer declaring the Father's love for her and commanding all pain to leave. She immediately commented that it felt a bit better and less stiff and I asked if I could pray some more. After praying a second time she looked at me with surprise and said, 'It's a lot better, all the stiffness has gone! How did you do that?' I said, 'It wasn't me, it was Jesus and He loves you so much. Do you know Him?' She said something about remembering learning about God at school but then the changing room door opened and the conversation came to a close as she had to deal with a customer. Even though I didn't get to chat to her further I know that day His Kingdom drew near and she got to encounter the God who loves her and knew her physical need. Everywhere we go we meet people who are in some kind of pain whether it's emotional, mental or physical, and it's not always visible, but the hope we have in Jesus is what they need. Christ in us.

My friend was working in a café for a while. Choosing not to join in with gossip and occasional backbiting amongst staff she stood out because instead she showed unconditional love and kindness. One staff member noticed this which led her to ask my friend questions about what she believes. She stood out because of the light that she carries. I have another friend who works as a radiographer at a hospital and she regularly has opportunities to bring hope and peace, often through a hug or kind words to people who are anxious when coming for x-rays. My daughter Hannah, a mum of four, has naturally befriended many mums, both in the school playground and just in her day-to-day life. One mum she met at the health visitor's clinic whilst having their babies weighed; they noticed they had the same buggy and just started chatting. Through an ongoing friendship this mum began coming to church with Hannah, attended an Alpha Course and, soon after, gave her life to Jesus. Since then her husband has also become a Christian and now they, too are reaching out to others with the love of Jesus.

When Jesus told us to go into the world and make disciples, He meant for us to shine in every place we go. Paul writes in 2 Corinthians 2:15, *'We are the aroma of Christ to God amongst those who are being saved and among those who are perishing.'* For some people this aroma of Christ in us will offend but for others this sweet aroma will draw them to God and they will want to know Him too. God knows those who are being saved and as Peter reminds us in 2 Peter 3:9, *'The Lord . . . is patient toward you, not wishing that any should perish.'* We carry the light of Jesus by the Holy Spirit and wherever we go we bring a light greater than the darkness around us. Everywhere Paul went he shone the light of the gospel even though not everyone could see it.

God's glory will always shine. His radiance and His brilliance are not dependent on our response to Him. God doesn't need to prove Himself because HE IS. The psalmist says, *'The heavens declare the glory of God, and the sky above proclaims his handiwork. Day to day pours out speech, and night to night reveals knowledge. There is no speech, nor are there words, whose voice is not heard. Their voice goes out through all the earth, and their words to the end of the world'* (Psalm 19:1-4). God, the creator of the universe, is on display for all to see.

There is a wonderful true story of a man who was having a bath and, as he lay there looking at the trees outside his window, he was struck by the variety of green colours amongst the leaves and thought there must be a God. He got out of the bath and looking up the nearest church, he went along, attended an Alpha Course and gave his life to Jesus. This man, called Jason, is now part of our church family.

God's desire to reveal Himself to us and to pursue us is so much greater than our ability to seek Him.

I love reading and hearing stories of people who have professed to be atheists and then have come to realise that not only is

God real but that He actually loves them. Sir Anthony Hopkins[3] says he was plagued by self-doubt, feelings of inadequacy and fear of failure and was both an atheist and alcoholic for many years until he decided he had had enough. Whilst in recovery someone asked him the question, 'Why don't you trust in God?' From that moment on, through a change of thinking, he got free from his addiction and began a search to know God for himself. He now says about atheism, 'Being an atheist must be like living in a closed cell with no windows.' As I have shared in a previous chapter, my discovery of God being real came as I encountered unconditional love in a way I had never experienced it before and I wanted to know it for myself. I began asking the question 'What is it these people have that I don't have?' I was drawn to the aroma of Christ in them. God is light and it is impossible for darkness to extinguish the light. As we are in Him, we are light and we are bound to shine. Our lives become an invitation for people to know and experience Jesus, the true light that has come into the world.

Do you know that God designed you to live this naturally supernatural life? That we can expect to see the miraculous in our everyday lives because we were designed with the miraculous in mind? Jesus said, *'Truly, truly, I say to you, whoever believes in me will also do the works that I do; and greater works than these will he do, because I am going to the Father. Whatever you ask in my name, this I will do, that the Father may be glorified in the Son. If you ask me anything in my name, I will do it'* (John 14:12-14). Learning to live like Jesus is letting His love shine brightly through us. Isaiah 60:1-3 says, *'Arise, shine, for your light has come, and the glory of the LORD has risen upon you . . . nations shall come to your light, and kings to the brightness of your rising.'* We have been enlightened and now we can shine like stars.

Before we move on it's worth asking ourselves how we are doing at simply shining. To help us at King's Arms Church[4] we teach various tools which enable us in learning to be disciples.

For every tool we have a symbol easily recognised as being on a computer keyboard. One symbol is 'turning up the brightness'. This is a reminder to us that as followers of Jesus we are called to shine brightly as His children wherever we are and we regularly hear stories of people doing this in their places of work, in their families and local communities as well as out on the streets.

I wonder what 'turning up the brightness' looks like for you? It may be realising afresh how loved by God you are, knowing you are a son or daughter first before you do anything for Him. It may be expecting God to actually move through you and stepping out and saying, 'Excuse me . . .'! For all of us it's becoming more aware of opportunities wherever we are and being ready for God to interrupt our day. Maybe when you are out, why not ask God the question I asked, 'Who do You want me to show Your love to today?' Then see who the Holy Spirit draws your attention to or who seems drawn to you and see what the Father will do.

CHAPTER FOUR

A Kingdom People

Whenever you enter a town and they
receive you, eat what is set before you.
Heal the sick in it and say to them,
'The kingdom of God has come near to you.'

Luke 10:8

It was my friend's first full day of supply teaching and God did something amazing! When I heard her story it really impacted me not only because of my friend's extraordinary courage but because it is such a great example of what it means to see God's Kingdom come in the 'everyday' of life. I asked her to send it to me.

She wrote,

In the lesson after lunch, I was timetabled to take a Philosophy lesson for a Year 5 class. The outline I was given for the lesson was 'to look at the life of Jesus and storyboard it, including key people and places'. I laughed and thought, 'This has to be God!' I was very excited and so I texted my friend before the lesson. She texted back saying, 'Preach the gospel, girl! Go for it and let me know how many get saved!'

I'd watched *Furious Love* and *The Finger of God* DVDs[1] the night before and felt impacted by Heidi Baker[2] getting the children to pray for a man and seeing the man totally healed. I was also impacted by the need to love others and preach the gospel accompanied by signs and wonders. In my head I started to dream about how fun it would be if a whole load of kids got healed and people were saved, then I thought, 'I can't do that, that would be crazy!'

I began the lesson by sharing with the kids how excited I was that we got to talk about my favourite subject – Jesus. We began by talking about who Jesus was, where He came from and why He was sent. We went on to think of lots of examples in the Bible of miracles Jesus did in His life and then we unpacked the whole gospel together in quite a lot of detail; the kids were hooked! I explained that because I believe in Jesus, He is alive in me and that He is eager to bring God's Kingdom on the earth. Then I asked the question, 'Do you want Jesus to reveal Himself to you today?' to which the whole class very excitedly said, 'YES!' 'Oh no', I thought, 'what am I saying?' There was no going back now! I asked if anyone had any pain or sickness in their body. A boy with a bruised hand piped up so I asked the kid next to him to put his hand on the boy's. I prayed once but there was no change. Lots of kids laughed. I said, 'That's ok, let's pray again and see what happens.' This time I got all the kids to come around and put their hands on his and then repeat after me, 'Jesus, we thank You that You heal, please reveal Yourself to us. Bring Your Kingdom here. We command pain and bruising in this hand to go in the name of Jesus.' The boy then started poking and hitting his hand. All the pain had gone!

Another kid then asked me to pray for his ankle, and after praying a few times he said, 'The pain is gone!' I then asked who else in the class wanted to be healed. Most put their hands up! I got the kids to ask the person closest to them who needed healing, where the pain was. I then got them to repeat after me, 'Thank you, Jesus, that you heal. Please show yourself to us,' and I got them to command the specific pain to go in the name of Jesus.

About half the kids who responded for healing were healed of various things, ranging from back pain to knee pain to bruises that didn't hurt any more. The other half complained that they weren't healed. I told them, 'I have no idea why Jesus heals some and not others but I know He loves to heal, so let's pray again,' and more children were healed!

Some of those who weren't healed started to come up to me rather disappointed. A boy with a mouth ulcer came up to me and very bluntly complained, 'Jesus didn't heal me.' I asked the kid next to him to pray. I told him to put his hand on the boy's shoulder and repeat a prayer after me, commanding the pain to go. At the first time of praying, the pain got less. I said in disbelief, 'Are you for real?' He said, 'Yep' and we prayed again for total healing. The boy sharply said the pain had gone. Again I said, 'Really?' and he said, 'Yep, it's gone.' So I told him to make sure and check it out. He stuck his finger in his mouth, started rubbing around his gum and declared, 'The ulcer is gone!'

At this point I was a bit nervous that the kids hadn't done their work so I stopped the remaining kids asking me to pray for them, and asked the class to do their storyboards. As the lesson was drawing to a close by this point, I was reminded of the text I'd received saying, 'Let me know how many are saved,' I thought to myself, 'I can't do that, can I?' Suddenly I found myself saying to the children, 'Jesus revealed Himself to us today. How many of you now believe in Jesus and want to accept Him into your life?' Lots of them said a very loud and confident 'YES!' I emphasised the fact it was a choice and they didn't have to pray the prayer, but if they wanted to then they should close their eyes and repeat after me a prayer accepting Jesus into their lives. They repeated after me with such passion and conviction, it surprised me! After praying, I ended the lesson by telling the class about the relationship they can now have with

Jesus. I then invited them to the 9–11s kids' work I led at King's Arms, and took a record of who was healed and who prayed the prayer to follow Jesus. Fifteen kids said they were healed and seventeen kids said they asked Jesus into their life for the very first time! COME ON, JESUS! As I left the classroom I was blown away by what had happened. God's Kingdom had come in an amazing way!

Signs and wonders point people to Jesus

This is God's Kingdom on display! The Holy Spirit loves to draw close when we make much of Jesus. When we love people and share the gospel we can expect signs and wonders to follow. Signs of God's presence and power confirm the gospel and point people to Jesus. When I pray for people for healing I often ask them whilst praying if they are experiencing anything in their body. They may or may not but sometimes people say they feel warmth or even intense heat. This is the power and healing presence of Jesus. I have even heard stories of people who said they felt the part of their body that needed healing moving inside them as God was doing internal surgery. God's presence and power to heal is a beautiful sign and wonder of who He is. It's a tangible sign of God's goodness.

In Mark's gospel we read, *'And these signs will accompany those who believe: in my name they will cast out demons; they will speak in new tongues; they will pick up serpents with their hands; and if they drink any deadly poison, it will not hurt them; they will lay their hands on the sick, and they will recover'* (Mark 16:17-18). After Jesus had spoken this and was taken up into heaven we read the disciples went out and preached everywhere while the Lord worked with them and confirmed the message by accompanying signs.

Jesus told His friends, *'Whenever you enter a town and they receive you, eat what is set before you. Heal the sick in it and say to them, "The Kingdom of God has come near to you"'*

(Luke 10:8-9). As He spoke about His Kingdom, Jesus revealed that His rule and reign would often be displayed through signs wonders and the miraculous. As His friends and followers we too carry this same power and authority. Miracles were normal for Jesus, they became normal for the disciples, and I believe as part of sharing the good news of the Kingdom they are meant to become normal for us too. His Kingdom is ever advancing and it is wonderful when we get to see a manifestation of God's presence and glory on the earth. I saw this just recently in the hairdressers.

Lana had cut my hair a few times before and as I arrived she seemed pleased to see me. She is a lovely warm-hearted lady and always ready for a chat. On previous occasions we had talked a little about God and she had asked me if I went to a 'born again' church and whether I was 'that sort of a Christian'. On this occasion, however, Lana began talking to me about the painful arthritis she had in her hands and feet and how she'd had it for many years. She showed me one of her hands, which was now slightly clawed. Clearly she was in pain but as she didn't want to take morphine patches, she said, 'It's just something I have to live with.'

Whenever anyone says that, I feel a righteous indignation rise up in me because I know that's what the devil wants people to believe; instead I know God wants to show people His compassion and that nothing is impossible for Him. I asked Lana if anyone had ever prayed for her and she said she remembered someone praying for her once many years ago but said nothing much had happened. I began to tell her stories of people I have seen healed by Jesus, including two ladies with arthritis who a group of us had prayed for in our prayer café in Costa coffee shop. I told her that it's Jesus who heals because He loves us and mentioned that I could pray for her too. She didn't say anything, we carried on chatting, and then she left me awhile as she cut and blow-dried a lady's hair next to me. I didn't think too much more about our conversation apart from wishing I had been able to pray for her and saying that to God.

Later, as Lana was washing my hair at the sink, she suddenly said from behind me, 'Were you praying for me? You were praying for me weren't you?' I was a bit taken aback. I wasn't sure how to answer.

I had certainly been thinking about how I wanted to pray for her. So I settled for saying, 'Yes, I was thinking about what you'd said and talking to God, why?' Lana said, 'Well, my hand is better, so much better! I was able to blow-dry that lady's hair without any pain and it has never felt this good!'

As I returned to my seat, still processing what had just happened, I said, 'I'd love to pray for your hand.' She said, 'But it's a lot better!' Excited to see what else God would do, I said, 'That's wonderful, can I pray that all the pain goes away?' She held out her hand to me and I prayed, commanding every bit of pain to leave and not return. I saw in her face how moved she was and she continued saying it was so much better. When it was time to pay and leave I checked in with Lana about her hand and she said again, 'I'm so amazed, this has never happened; I've never been without pain before.' As I smiled at her, she leaned in closer and told me that as she'd driven to work that morning she had said out loud, 'Not even an animal should have to go through this much pain!' I knew immediately in my spirit God had heard her desperate cry and I replied, 'God knew and He loves you, Lana.' With Sundays being her day off, I said before leaving, 'Lana, why don't you come to church one week?' She asked the times of the services and said, 'I may well surprise you, it's been a long time since I've been to church.'

What struck me was that Jesus didn't even need me to pray for Lana, God had already heard and answered her cry. That day, as I shared stories of His goodness, I got to see His beautiful Kingdom on display.

What the Bible says about the Kingdom

At the start of His ministry Jesus went into the synagogue, as was the custom, and a scroll was handed to Him to read. As

He opened the scroll He read, '*The Spirit of the Lord is upon me, because he has anointed me to proclaim good news to the poor. He has sent me to proclaim liberty to the captives and recovering of sight to the blind, to set at liberty those who are oppressed, to proclaim the year of the Lord's favour*' (Luke 4:18-19). As Jesus finished reading, He rolled up the scroll and handed it back and with every eye fastened on Him, He said, '*Today this scripture has been fulfilled in your hearing*' (v.21). These words of prophecy in Isaiah 61, seven hundred years before, had come to pass. Jesus was the fulfilment of this Kingdom manifesto that Isaiah had been prophesying about. The Jews had lived with an expectation of a Messiah who would put everything right. They'd hoped for a powerful ruler and one who would overthrow their Roman oppressors but when Jesus came He ushered in a completely different kind of Kingdom. Contrary to the expectations of most people in His day, Jesus brought a Kingdom that wasn't one of power grabbing or driven by violence but a Kingdom of love. It was a Kingdom of grace and not law, one of humility and not pride and a Kingdom that was for all men and not just the Jews. The way Jesus entered Jerusalem on a young colt demonstrated this kind of Kingdom He had come to establish. Instead of coming as a conquering general, He came as the Prince of Peace. He came proclaiming love, forgiveness, healing and deliverance. Jesus came for the poor and the oppressed, those who were outcasts and on the edge of society. He came opposing the proud and lifting up the weak, and He came not to be served but to lay down His life for us.

The importance of the Kingdom cannot be overstated. In the gospels alone there are a hundred references to the Kingdom in Jesus' ministry. It was Jesus' main message and central to everything He ministered. When He preached and when He healed the sick and did miracles, He told people the Kingdom of God was at hand. Signs and wonders were a visible and tangible demonstration that His rule and reign had come near to them in anticipation of that day when all the earth will flourish under the reign of God. As Jesus went about proclaiming this good news of the Kingdom, He demonstrated it with many signs and wonders. The sick were healed, blind eyes were opened, the oppressed set free and the dead were raised. In Matthew 24:14 Jesus said, *'And this gospel of the kingdom will be proclaimed throughout the whole world as a testimony to all nations, and then the end will come.'*

Bringing the Kingdom is learning to live like Jesus. Isaiah 61 shows us what our Kingdom influence looks like. Let's take a look at some of the signs of Jesus' Kingdom.

His presence

As Moses prepared to lead the children of Israel out of Egypt he prayed to God saying, *'If your presence will not go with me, do not bring us up from here'* (Exodus 33:15). Moses knew that without God's presence they were doomed. God told him, *'My presence will go with you, and I will give you rest'* (v.14). What a promise! He was saying to them and to us, too, I am enough for you; I will provide for you everything you need. God led His people by a pillar of cloud by day and a pillar of fire by night. How awesome it must have been to witness God's manifest presence in this way every day. Even though we now have the promise of God's presence in us and don't depend on a physical manifestation to follow, God still wants to show Himself to us, and often in surprising ways. There have been a few times where I have looked down at my hands or arms and seen gold dust appear; a visible reminder and glimpse of His glory. Signs like these always fill me with joy and excitement because I know they are just a foretaste of what we will see one day when we meet Him.

Wherever we go we carry His presence with us. This means that wherever God's Kingdom is on display we can expect the Holy Spirit to be near. It's a beautiful thing to see the Holy

Spirit both flowing through people and also coming to rest on people. Sometimes His manifest presence is like a stillness that envelops, and sometimes His presence comes in a visibly powerful way that may cause people to shake or fall down or to laugh with joy. There are accounts of all of these manifestations in the Bible. 'Falling' in Ezekiel 1:28, Daniel 8:17 and Revelation 1:17; 'trembling' or 'shaking' in Jeremiah 23:9 and Habakkuk 3:16; and loss of strength in Daniel 10:8-10. The important thing, of course, is not the nature of the manifestation but our encounter with God.

I once prayed for a girl who was suffering with panic attacks. As I looked at her I remember I felt overwhelmed with the certainty of God's love for her and I had few words. I simply told her, 'Jesus doesn't want you to have them anymore.' I didn't need to pray or lay hands on her because in that moment the Holy Spirit flooded her with His peace and I just got to stand back and watch. It was extraordinary and powerful as she encountered Jesus, the Prince of Peace. A few weeks later she came and told me she hadn't had any more attacks and was now sitting near the front of the church instead of at the back, where she used to sit before, ready to run out if needed. I have seen freedom come to people who at the start were crying and then as the Holy Spirit fell on them began laughing as they encountered His joy. His presence can come both powerfully and gently.

I remember another time when I was on a ministry trip in Zambia and a few of us went into a very poor area. To give an idea of the poverty, there were boys playing football but instead of a ball they had rags they'd tied together. They were laughing and having so much fun. I remember being struck by the love of this very poor community of people, who were quickly finding oilcans and pieces of broken wood for us to sit on – anything they had in their eagerness to be hospitable. After praying first for a man and seeing Jesus take pain away from his leg, he then asked us to pray for his little boy who had chest problems. As I laid my hands on him I immediately sensed the presence of God and noticed the little boy swaying as he, too, was encountering His presence. It was a precious moment seeing the richness of God being poured out in the midst of such poverty. I realised in that moment I was witnessing God's Kingdom. Jesus loves to come to those who are poor. He brings good news to the poor.

Healing

Healing is a sign of God's Kingdom and we know because Jesus went about healing all who were sick. People received healing on the inside and on the outside. Jesus told His disciples, *'Heal the sick . . . and say to them, "The Kingdom of God has come near to you"'* (Luke 10:9).

Some friends and I have the amazing privilege of praying for people in a Costa store in our town which I'll tell you more about in another chapter. One day, when two ladies came into the café we noticed one was hobbling and so we asked her if she would like us to pray for her. Carol said she was sure we couldn't do anything as she'd had this problem of arthritis for many years. Stepping out in faith, I said to her 'We can't, but Jesus can heal you!' I remember thinking, wow, that was a bold statement, yet I knew I believed it to be true. What happened next was truly miraculous: after praying we saw Jesus take all the pain away from Carol's right hip. She was so amazed she turned to her friend and said, 'You should let them pray for you!' Her friend Janet suffered with severe back pain because of scoliosis and she also said she was doubtful anything could change. She was in a lot of pain and told us how that very morning she had decided to stop taking her medication as it was upsetting her stomach. My friend Tim then spoke up and told Janet that he had actually been healed of scoliosis himself! After hearing his story, Janet cautiously agreed to Tim praying for her. As we asked her to check out her back to see if there was any change, she began to tell us that she was sure there wouldn't be but then had to interrupt herself as she felt a click in her back and realised all the pain had left. We looked at one another in awe of what God was doing in front of us. Janet was amazed too and was now asking if we could pray for Carol's left hip. A thought suddenly popped into my head, which I believed was Holy Spirit inspired: I suggested to Janet she might like to pray for Carol having just seen what Jesus had done. Janet agreed and, copying our words, she prayed a simple prayer saying, 'Jesus, please heal my friend and take her pain away.' I think you can guess what happened!

That day two ladies who didn't know Jesus or believe in His power encountered freedom from pain and we got to then sit and talk with them about who Jesus is and His love for them. This is the good news of the gospel. As we lay hands on the sick we see God's Kingdom released and Satan's work demolished.

Salvation and deliverance

Salvation belongs to God and is given to men. When the Kingdom comes, salvation comes and brings freedom to those who are bound by sin, fear, shame, addictions and everything that holds people captive. It's wonderful seeing freedom come to those who put their faith in Christ.

In the same coffee shop one day we had the joy of praying with a young man who came in very distressed. David told us his story. Whilst in prison he had experienced God's love in a tangible way and noticed over the following three days how God kept answering his prayers. Shortly after this, someone in the prison gave him an Islamic book to read and gradually he forgot about the experience he'd had in the prison chapel. Meeting us that day brought it all back for him and David told us he was afraid he had blasphemed the Holy Spirit. I remember being taken aback by his use of that phrase. What had led him to believe this I don't know, but we got to reassure David of God's love, how God had never left him and there, in the coffee shop, he repented and received Jesus into his heart for the very first time. It was a precious moment and I asked Russ, one of our team members, if he'd like to pray for David for the Holy Spirit to fill him. We both watched as God's peace fell on him. He was completely still with his eyes closed as though he didn't want to move. I could see out of the corner of my eye a lady at a nearby table watching us pray for him and I briefly wondered what she thought was going on.

I discovered later that Russ had never prayed for anyone to receive the Holy Spirit before and I was reminded of the joy of partnering in the gospel. God proclaims liberty to the captives and the opening of the prison to those who are bound.

Comfort

Jesus brings comfort to those who mourn. Losing someone really hurts and often all we want is to be alone. Jesus Himself knew what it was like to lose good friends. He wept when Lazarus died and when He heard John the Baptist had been beheaded Jesus wanted to be alone to grieve. There are many ways we encounter loss, whether that's the loss of a loved one, the loss of a parent not being there, or a feeling of having been abandoned or mistreated. In times like these there can be a very real temptation to turn to other places to seek comfort, even to harden our hearts, but Jesus wants us to come to Him. He identifies with our loss and our pain because He has experienced it for us. He has experienced the full gamut of emotions. One look at Jesus suffering on the cross and we know He understands our pain. He was rejected, He was mocked and spat on, He suffered abuse and torture at the hands of those He'd come to save, and He was even abandoned by many of His friends who were afraid to stand with Him.

Sometimes I have asked people in the street this question: 'If God could do a miracle for you what would you ask Him to do?' Many have said they would ask for God to bring a close relative or friend back to them who has died. Instead of just saying that's not possible, it has been an opportunity to show compassion and pray for them to know God's supernatural comfort. I remember praying for a lady in the street who had recently been widowed after fifty years of being married to her best friend. I could only try to imagine the sense of loss she was feeling but I knew God understood. She began to cry as I prayed for her and, even though it was painful and emotional for her, I came away believing that God had drawn near to her to show her His very real comfort in the midst of her pain and loss.

I have a friend who is an airline steward and does long-haul flights. Asking a lady in business class why she was travelling to the UK she broke down as she told him she was coming for her daughter's funeral. My friend spent the next few hours listening and comforting her. Offering to pray for her, he had a picture come into his head of her with horses and of a ranch. Even though he didn't share it with her he heard later from a colleague who had asked the lady what she did that it was exactly that: she owned horses on a ranch. God knows us intimately and wants to comfort us. *'He heals the broken-hearted and binds up their wounds'* (Psalm 147:3).

Justice

Throughout the world we experience injustice on many levels. On a global scale this might be as a result of corrupt governments that wrongfully imprison people. It may be because of war or violence causing people to be forced to leave their homes and become refugees. And there can also be injustice in the work place or injustice within the family or within marriages or relationships. God hates injustice and where Jesus reigns, justice reigns. For the Bible says, *'The LORD is a God of justice; blessed are all those who wait for him'* (Isaiah 30:18). We know that one day all wrongs will be made right.

Peace

When God's Kingdom comes His peace comes because He is the Prince of Peace. His peace can come in the midst of a storm. When His peace comes it is like no other peace; it surpasses our understanding.

A while back I was part of a team visiting a church to minister during a weekend's Father Heart Conference.[3] We'd been praying for lots of people during the last morning and it was nearly time for us to leave. A girl who I had seen struggling throughout the weekend came towards me. I knew that she had lots of physical problems as well as issues with anxiety and depression. Tired and feeling a bit empty, I didn't really want to pray for any more people. With very little faith and not much compassion I prayed a short prayer. Immediately God came to her in such a powerful way; His presence and peace seemed to completely envelop her. I didn't know what God was doing but clearly He was doing something wonderful and I felt humbled as she kept thanking me for praying. It was a powerful reminder that He is made perfect in our weakness and so much bigger than our frailty.

Joy

I love how children show us what joy looks like. They are full of awe and continual amazement at what is going on around them. Even if they get temporarily offended, they quickly forget because they are too busy having fun. We can learn a lot from children, which is why Jesus told the disciples to welcome the Kingdom like a child.

Joy is a sign of God's Kingdom. Isaiah prophesied about the oil of joy and Jesus turning our sadness into gladness. Comparing God's salvation to a well, Isaiah said, *'With joy you will draw water from the wells of salvation'* (Isaiah 12:3). King David had already tasted this refreshing water of joy and when it came to his plea for mercy and forgiveness, he cried out to God, *'Restore to me the joy of your salvation'* (Psalm 51:12).

Happiness is a fluctuating emotion determined by circumstances, but joy is something much deeper. Joy is not an emotion but an attitude of the heart. We all have and will go through hard times and feel despondent yet it's possible that in the midst of the worst of storms we can encounter deep joy. When one of our grandbabies, Eli, was ill in hospital after coming through a very difficult pregnancy and premature birth, many of us were praying. It had been like a rollercoaster ride, especially for his mum and dad. I remember one Sunday when things were not looking good that instead of feeling fear I was feeling joyful, and it almost seemed inappropriate. As friends reached out in love I could see their anxiety yet somehow it wasn't touching me because inside I had such a deep certainty of God's goodness, it was something quite supernatural. I'm glad to say that Eli, who is now nine years old, is a very strong, healthy young boy. As the psalmist says, *'Weeping may tarry for the night, but joy comes with the morning'* (Psalm 30:5).

The Kingdom of God is both now and not yet

We know God's Kingdom is ever advancing even though we don't yet see it in its fullness. We don't yet see every person we pray for healed or see the results of all of our prayers this side of heaven but Jesus was clear about how we should pray. He said when you pray, pray like this, *'Your kingdom come, your will be done, on earth as it is in heaven'* (Matthew 6:10). We know that when Jesus returns there will be a new heaven and a new earth and He will make all things new. Every tear will be wiped away. There will be no more sadness or pain or death.

As we live in the interim of the Kingdom being both now and not yet, God has shown us how to live from a place of faith and hope. Listening to Bill Johnson speaking about hearing from God, I was struck by this wonderful statement he made. He said,

'Whenever God does a miracle or something extraordinary in our lives He is awakening our affections for an unseen world. The natural and the supernatural are not in conflict but co-operating together with us as His agents connecting the two.'[4]

We are Kingdom cultural transformers

Being certain of God's goodness is what brings cultural transformation. Our Kingdom influence may look different for each of us. For some it may be in the church leading and equipping others, for some it will be in family life investing in children and raising up world changers, and for others it will be in the marketplace in our places of work or other areas of influence. I want to tell you about some people I know who are doing just this in many different spheres.

I have a couple of friends who are leadership development coaches. They meet with clients who are business leaders and either overtly or covertly they get to pass on Kingdom values. They know that Kingdom values will bring harmony, unity and good working relationships to the businesses they represent. In a world where business can often be competitive and hard-nosed, they are passing on an example of leadership and good practice that seeks to honour and lift others up in the workplace. Their passion is to 'change the face of leadership' to one that reflects Jesus. Karen is one of these coaches and she told me how as part of her coaching sessions she often talks about emotional intelligence: how past experiences can influence our responses to others. One time one of her clients announced that he did not just need to learn about emotional intelligence but also spiritual intelligence. She recognised this as an appointment only God could have orchestrated. After leading him through repentance and deliverance from his unhealthy involvement in a spiritualist church, she then had the privilege of leading him to Christ and being filled with the Holy Spirit. This was all in a two-hour, one-to-one coaching session!

Andrea works for the NHS and, noticing the long hours and dedication of her team in a very demanding job, decided to create a 'Shout Out' board. It was a board where team members could post sticky notes applauding, encouraging and thanking other members of staff on a regular basis. She has noticed what a positive effect it has had already on the morale of the team. My friend isn't the team leader but she knows that encouragement is the culture of God's Kingdom and that is what she carries and demonstrates wherever she goes.

I have another friend who is a GP and who is bringing the Kingdom in her surgery. As she partners with Jesus asking Him how to help people who come to her, God is giving her words of knowledge that have often led to people's breakthrough both physically and emotionally. My friend is passionate and courageous to see God's Kingdom come and to see heaven invade our healthcare system. She shared the following story with me.

I like to ask the Holy Spirit for creative ways of helping people access the healing Father heart of God. One idea came to me to prepare some pieces of broken pottery with significant 'Kingdom' words on for people to connect with. On one occasion I was with a lady who came in, very low in mood and heartbroken. It was a year on from the death of her daughter who had been in her twenties. This young woman, who had been unwell with serious illnesses, had been taken advantage of by her carer, a much older man, who used her benefits and sold off many of her pain medications for profit. The mother felt helpless to intervene, and was recently bereaved herself from the death of her husband, and son-in-law. She told me she hated this carer with everything in her being and could never forgive him, but at the same time asked me to help her out of this dark place.

I thought of my pottery pieces and had a lightning nudge from the Holy Spirit to show her all of them and ask her which one she would like to pick out. As she picked out the one marked

GO

'Freedom' I knew we would have to talk about forgiveness. I explained that the only way for her to receive her own freedom was to forgive this carer. I explained what forgiveness actually is: that it is relinquishing the right to be judge, and allowing God His rightful place to be the just judge. We prayed, and in that moment the Holy Spirit was present to enable her to hand over her pain and offence to Jesus. As I prayed about Christ's suffering and humiliation on the cross for her and for everyone, I saw Jesus come into her place of vulnerability and heal her heart. It was a beautiful moment right there in the midst of a chaotic busy morning surgery. She took the piece of pottery home, and with tears in her eyes she hugged me. The next day I received a message from her. She said, 'Thank you for my freedom.'

Carole, a friend from my previous church who lives in Brighton, is a beauty therapist. One time I felt God say that as she was doing treatments to expect that God would sometimes speak to her for her clients, giving her words of knowledge. At the time she said she couldn't imagine that ever happening. Many months later Carole messaged me and said, 'I remember you once telling me this and I didn't believe it. Now I often sense the Holy Spirit near and sometimes God gives me words for my clients.'

I know others who are bringing the Kingdom through the avenues of media, the arts, in the political arena, in prison governing and in education.

Whether our influence is big or small, what we carry will transform the culture around us because we carry the presence of the King. This is Kingdom cultural transformation.

Jesus said He would build the church and He called us to extend His Kingdom. Do you know that this is your heavenly assignment? It's the reason you and I are on the earth in our generation and it is what the church is meant to look like.

The world is hungry for an encounter with Jesus and it's through the church that His Kingdom is on display. Not through a rule-based religion or denominationalism but through an authentic demonstration of His love, power and goodness. People need to experience the embrace of a loving Father. Often people have only experienced a religion of legalism – a set of rules and behaviours they just can't keep – and it has left them empty. Jesus spoke out against this kind of religion. This kind of religion says 'reach up to God and try harder'. Instead, God reached down to us and said, *'Come to me, all who labour and are heavy laden, and I will give you rest'* (Matthew 11:28).

We see this when people encountered Jesus. Because He is love, that's what people encountered. It was love that led people like Zacchaeus to repentance and to follow Him. Jesus didn't first say to Zacchaeus you must stop cheating people and pay back what you owe and then follow me. Instead, Jesus said I must come to your house today and eat with you. As Zacchaeus encountered God's love it led him to follow Jesus and change the way he lived (Luke 19:1-10). It's God's kindness that leads to repentance, and not the other way around.

When Jesus taught us to pray for His Kingdom to come on earth, as it is in heaven, I believe His desire was for us to live with this expectation of His Kingdom breaking out around us. The world desperately needs to see and know who God is. To know that He is loving, kind and full of compassion to all He has made. People need to see that although God is holy and we don't deserve His grace, He is not distant or remote. That He loves us so much He sent His only Son to show us His great love and mercy. We as ambassadors of heaven get to show people what the Father is like as we distribute His peace, as we heal the sick, as we bring words of hope to those in despair and as we preach the gospel. Jesus said He would build the church and He sent us to preach the good news of the Kingdom. I wonder whether you would say that being an ambassador of the Kingdom is your main preoccupation? The Kingdom is the absolute centre of who we are. It's our divine assignment to bring the reality of His Kingdom to the earth. I love what Alan Scott writes in his book *Scattered Servants*. He says, 'We are sent the same way Jesus Himself was sent, in glory, authority, humility, and vulnerability. The church is the group of people sent to bring life to cities and regions and nations. God doesn't send the lost into the church, He sends the found into the world.'[5]

I believe we are living in days where we are seeing more and more signs of God's Kingdom breaking out around us as we take the message of Jesus outside of the church. I sense God is bringing something of a paradigm shift and calling the church back to her true identity, reminding us that we are first and foremost a Kingdom people.

I encourage you. Today go and bless people! Love people whether that's through the kindness of your smile, your touch, or your words. Distribute life, hope, peace and healing. Reach up and pull down from heaven as you pray for people because you know who He is. Invite people to receive Jesus today to receive everlasting life; life in all its fullness.

CHAPTER FIVE

Moved by Love

The Lord is good to all;
he has compassion on all he has made.

Psalm 145:9 (NIV)

Everywhere Jesus went He was moved by love. Even when He was tired, grieving or preferring to be alone with His Father, He often chose to minister to needy crowds pressing in on Him. We see this so beautifully in Matthew 14. Jesus had just heard of the death of John the Baptist and went off in a boat to be alone. As He reached the shore Jesus saw a great crowd coming towards Him and, instead of withdrawing, He was moved with compassion and healed all who were sick. As we see in Luke 5, Jesus prioritised being with His Father but there were also many times, even when He was tired, that He chose to minister to people. Jesus loved people into the Kingdom. He served people with full acceptance, meeting them where they were. He ministered to their immediate needs, while all the time addressing their greatest need, which was to know Him and to follow Him.

It was Jesus' love that upset the culture. His love often broke the rules. He healed people on the Sabbath, He forgave sin, and He honoured women and children. In first-century Jewish culture a woman's place was in the home. Women were responsible for bearing and raising children, and keeping house. Some taught that women shouldn't even leave the home except to go to the synagogue. Women had no voice and were vulnerable and overlooked, which sadly still happens in parts of our world today. Jesus didn't treat women this way. He didn't see them as inferior but instead He loved and honoured them. He forgave the woman caught in adultery, He healed the woman who pressed through the crowds to touch Him, and He spoke with both the Samaritan and the Syrophoenician woman; all of which was completely counter cultural. Mary and Martha were amongst His closest friends. Jesus made a point of highlighting Mary who chose to sit at His feet and He also honoured Mary who poured expensive ointment over His feet to express her love and devotion. Many of Jesus' disciples were women. It was women who were the first to seek Him after His death and it was the women who He first showed Himself to after He had risen.

Jesus honoured children too. When they wanted to run to Jesus and the disciples tried to send them away, Jesus welcomed them. He not only blessed children, but also then turned and taught the disciples to imitate and learn from them also.

Jesus upset religious people by healing those who were outcasts, and who were considered unclean. He offended the leaders of the synagogue when He healed on the Sabbath the woman who had been bent over for eighteen years and the man born blind. Jesus challenged religious elitists and the self-righteous saying, *'Those who are well have no need of a physician, but those who are sick. I came not to call the righteous, but sinners'* (Mark 2:17).

In every way Jesus' standard of love was counter cultural. Those who were on the margins and overlooked dared to come to Him. The woman with the issue of blood, the lepers and the poorest of the poor all pursued Jesus. People who are the lost, the least and the last know they need help and Jesus is the one who always wants to lift them up. *'He raises the poor from the dust and lifts the needy from the ash heap'* (Psalm 113:7). God is close to the broken-hearted and His care for the poor is a major theme throughout the Bible. We have regularly seen this both on the streets and in the café.

Malcolm

Malcolm came to see us regularly in our prayer café in Costa. We were so thankful he no longer had panic attacks after we prayed for him and that we had the opportunity to lead him in a simple prayer to receive Jesus. Malcolm had many other health challenges though: a heart condition, chronic oedema and ulcers on his legs which needed regular dressing. We prayed for him many times for these and saw no change yet he continued coming asking us to pray. Malcolm's life sadly ended in hospital following pneumonia. My friend Tim was with him in his last few days, praying, reading scripture and singing over him, and I was with him just hours before he died. We saw some miracles along the way but sadly we didn't get to see Malcolm fully healed. We know he is now without pain and we trust that because of the kindness and mercy of Jesus he is now enjoying the Father's unconditional love. There is mystery and it feels costly loving when we don't always see what we long for.

One thing we can be certain of, is the Father's love is way bigger than we can understand or even imagine.

Simon

Simon is tormented by voices. He has told us that when he sits with us he feels better and not so alone. He doesn't stay long and is reluctant for us to pray for him but we get to love him, as Jesus would do.

Charlie

When we met Charlie he was looking for cigarette butts on the ground. Charlie is thirty-eight and has been hearing voices in his head since he was a young boy. His mother moved away when he was small and he was sent to boarding school because his father couldn't cope with him. He didn't want to speak about his father and turned away when we asked about him. His father had had so many women who had called themselves Charlie's 'mother' and we could feel his pain and rejection. We spent time with Charlie. We bought him some groceries and told him that he really mattered to God but he was carrying so much rejection it was hard for him to receive. He reluctantly let us pray for him before he went on his way and we saw moments of hope in his eyes when we spoke words about the Father's love for him.

Maria

Maria came in pushing a walking aid. We could see she was in need of physical healing but, as the conversation progressed, it became clear that God wanted to heal far more than just her physical body. She was weighed down with guilt, shame, self-hatred, loneliness, grief, and she admitted to self-harming regularly. She was convinced that she was ugly and unlovable. She told us that she believed in God but that she felt He saw her as a failure and a disappointment and that He could never want her. We told her how much the Father loved her and as we shared the gospel we spoke truth over her. We told Maria that there was a chair at God's banqueting table with her name on it. No one else could sit in it but her. It had always been there for her and the Father was just waiting for her to take her place at His table, and become part of His family. Maria knew about Jesus and what He had done for her and said she wanted to have that kind of relationship with God that we were speaking about and we then had the ultimate privilege of leading her to Jesus. As she finished praying and even before we asked for the Holy Spirit to fill her, Maria started laughing with joy. We asked her what was happening and she said she saw pure white rays of sunlight, which made her giggle. It was a beautiful moment. We prayed that the Holy Spirit would continue what

He had begun and heal her physically. She left us saying that she felt lighter and 'ten-feet tall'. Maria now comes regularly to church; she no longer needs her walking aid because Jesus has since healed her knees and she told me recently that she is now looking for work.

People are God's treasure

Every person is of immense value and worth in God's eyes. The psalmist says, '*The LORD is good to all; he has compassion on all he has made*' (Psalm 145:9 NIV).

I grew up around judgment and criticism. As kids we were forbidden to play with the children from the local estate because they were poor and we were discouraged generally from associating with people who were 'not like us'. Even though when I became a Christian I rejected this way of thinking, I often found myself battling with the same judgments. Behind a mask of seeming acceptance, inside I found I was looking down on people who were not like me. It is subtle but when people don't measure up to our standards or expectations we can be quick to withdraw or even reject one another. Instead, God wants us to value one another because God has made us each beautifully unique. I'm not like you and you're not like me. Imagine if God had made us all the same how dull that would be! God wants us to see the gold in one another and call it out as we honour and accept each other. This is learning to love as God loves us.

God sees us as the treasure He paid the highest price to redeem and as the church we should be known above all things for our love, welcoming people regardless of their background, race or lifestyle. There is a sacredness and dignity about all human life. We see this when a leper came kneeling before Jesus begging Him saying, '*If you will, you can make me clean*' (Matthew 8:2). He knew Jesus was his only hope. This man who had not known touch for a very long time, had only known rejection. Even in his question there was still fear and uncertainly. Jesus, who could have healed him with a word or even a thought, touched him because that is what he needed. Jesus settled the question in his heart as He said, *'I will; be clean'* (v.3). Full of compassion, Jesus showed this man love, acceptance and value.

How we love and accept one another is so important to God. We cannot win those we don't know how to love. God wants us to love people without an agenda and without pressure, not as projects or objects of our ministry but loving people for who they are.

Love is a choice and not just a feeling

Ever since I have asked God to show me His compassion for people and to make my heart like His, He has been putting opportunities in my path.

The town where I live is beautifully diverse. It is multicultural, made up of many ethnic groups. When I walk through our town the need can sometimes seem quite overwhelming because there are many who are poor. There are people sitting in doorways, there is a man I see with no legs and there are often people begging. Our town is known for its generosity – buying drinks, giving money and showing kindness to the poor – but it can feel costly. Sometimes the people who beg tell us stories that don't always add up. I know there have been many times I have been generous and my love has been unconditional but there have also been times I've hurried past with judgment in my heart.

I was on my way to the bank one day and a homeless man said, 'Please will you buy me some lunch?' There was demand in his tone but because I had just been asking God was there anything He wanted me to buy to give to someone, I recognised God was answering my prayer. I bought the man lunch; he didn't seem very thankful and I went on my way. Two days later I passed the same man. He was eating a Mars bar but at the same time calling out asking me if I'd buy him food. I looked at him and awkwardly said, 'I think I bought you some on Friday, do you remember?' As I walked on I immediately felt convicted as God showed me how I had been looking to feel appreciated for my generosity. Even though this man's attitude had revealed his orphan heart, so had it revealed mine also!

Learning Christ's way of love that we read in 1 Corinthians 13 is so provoking, a love that chooses to respond regardless of feelings. A love that doesn't grow weary in doing good to people, that doesn't expect anything in return, that doesn't seek its own comforts and that's willing to go the extra mile. I'm sure you'd agree it's a journey. I keep asking God that He will show me His compassion for people that sees beyond their brokenness. Instead of being overwhelmed by need I want to be overwhelmed by the love of Jesus because He really is the answer to everyone's need. Love like this is worth pushing through the awkward moments because sometimes it's the awkward that leads to the awesome!

Scott

I was out in our town centre with a few friends. We were looking to love people and share about Jesus. A lady approached me who seemed to be looking for a debate. She was angry towards God and I discovered she had lost an uncle who had been a key person in her life. I tried to share God's love with her but she walked away. For a while, feeling discouraged, I hung back from approaching anyone and I recognised the battle that was going on in my mind.

It was then that I saw a young man coming down the road walking very slowly on crutches. I said to God, 'If you want me to pray for him then please make him walk near where I am standing.' A few seconds later the young man moved across and I knew he would have to come right past me. I couldn't avoid him, so I stepped out and asked him what he had done to his foot, which was heavily bandaged.

Scott told me that he had come out of hospital just three days before, having had an operation on his Achilles tendon. 'Would you like me to pray for Jesus to heal it?' I asked. Scott's response was an enthusiastic, 'Yes, please!' and it took me by surprise. Scott was embarrassed for me to bend down to the ground to pray for his foot so I assured him that Jesus could heal his foot without me touching it. After praying once I asked if he could feel anything and he said he heard and felt a click. When I asked if he was in any pain he said no but that he would be if he put his foot on the ground, which he was very nervous to do.

Scott began to talk to me about his life and how he had been in prison. He said he was hungry and thirsty and I told him I wanted to buy him a drink and something to eat but that I'd love to pray for his foot one more time. He seemed so touched by my love for him and kept mentioning it.

I prayed for Scott's foot again and as I prayed I saw him gingerly trying to put it on the ground. I was still praying when, all of a sudden, Scott began swearing and saying there was no pain. He kept checking, putting his foot on the ground and doing it again and again. He told me excitedly that this was the second time something like this had happened to him. In prison a lady had prayed for him and he had been delivered from heroin addiction with no withdrawals. He said to me, 'She had the same power that you have.' I told him it was the power of Jesus and asked him if he knew Jesus. Scott said he had asked Jesus into his heart several times and how in prison he had attended Bible studies but he kept doing bad things and was very up and down.

Scott seemed overwhelmed by the love I was showing him and he kept thanking me. After I'd bought him something to eat and drink, a friend joined us and I left them talking so I could go and buy some socks and some plasters. Scott said a sock would be great to put on his foot now he could put it down on the ground. The plasters, which he said he didn't need, were for blisters I'd noticed he had from walking with crutches. As he reluctantly let me put the plasters on his hands I felt the tenderness of the Father towards him attending to the less visible hurts in his life. Soon after, Scott went on his way feeling loved and that day I experienced God's compassion for a complete stranger in a way I'd never encountered before.

When I got home I remembered what I had read in the morning from Isaiah 61 about bringing good news to the poor, binding up the broken-hearted, proclaiming freedom to the captives and bringing the oil of gladness instead of mourning and despair. I was so thankful to God that He chose me that day to display His Kingdom.

Annabel

I saw a woman come in late to the church meeting I was at in Manchester. She was struggling to walk because of her size. As God drew my attention to her I felt Him say, I want you to tell her how beautiful she is and that's what I see when I look at her; I see her beauty. As I felt God impressing this on me, I wanted to find her to tell her but it also felt awkward as I didn't know her. When the meeting finished I got chatting to Annabel over a coffee and then I shared what I'd felt God say. I didn't expand on it; I just told her exactly what God had said and I saw her eyes fill with tears. At the same time I noticed she was in some pain, which she told me was all down her right side. I offered to pray for her and, thanking God for His love for her, I commanded her right arm to be healed. Instantly we felt God's presence and she began excitedly waving her arm about as all the pain left. God showed me that day another glimpse of His kind and generous heart that is always seeing, always loving and always healing. As we display His compassion it attracts His presence.

Love always seeks to honour

Paul Manwaring writes:

> Beholding the glory of the Lord in the face of Christ involves the discipline of beholding Christ in the faces of one another (2 Corinthians 5:16). We must learn to say of the people we meet what Mother Teresa said of the poor she served: 'Each one of them is Jesus in disguise.' For as we learn to see Christ reflected in the faces of one another we begin to use the measure He used in honouring us to honour one another. This creates a flow of life, a flow of grace which brings what is unseen to the surface in our lives and closes the gap between earth and heaven.[1]

The depth of someone's love is shown through what it cost and our greatest example, of course, is Christ's love for us. Christ showed us the highest honour dying in our place and giving Himself completely for us. In the same measure, He has called us to honour one another as though Christ Himself.

One of the most provoking passages in the Bible to me is Matthew 25:35-40. Speaking about the final judgment, Jesus describes those who will inherit the Kingdom. He says,

> 'For I was hungry and you gave me food, I was thirsty and you gave me drink, I was a stranger and you welcomed me, I was naked and you clothed me, I was sick and you visited me, I was in prison and you came to me.' Then the righteous will answer him, saying, 'Lord, when did we see you hungry and feed you, or thirsty and give you drink? And when did we see you a stranger and welcome you, or naked and clothe you? And when did we see you sick or in

prison and visit you?' And the King will answer them, 'Truly, I say to you, as you did it to one of the least of these my brothers, you did it to me.'

Every day as we meet people, people who are created in God's image, we have an opportunity to show them honour. I have several friends who regularly provoke and inspire me by their example of compassion for people. One friend I know sat with a homeless man on the street who felt sick and held his hair back as he vomited. I was so provoked by her act of kindness and unconditional love.

I once got speaking to a lady in a café who had come in for her lunch break and who asked if she could join me at my table. As we talked she told me her job was in marketing and how she was glad to have left, in her words, 'the hard-nosed corporate world'. Now, instead of being motivated by money, she wanted to make a difference and was setting up her own marketing business and website to help people. This lady wasn't a Christian and yet she was displaying God's heart of justice and generosity. I hadn't referred to God at all but as I began to affirm and encourage her I saw tears in her eyes. I told her that the compassion and justice she was expressing came from God who had made her and who wanted her to know Him. This led to what she did and didn't believe and how she considered herself a Buddhist. I know she was impacted by what I'd said and before she left she said to me, 'I nearly didn't come into this café but I think I was meant to.'

Another time, my husband and I were out in Bedford seeing who we might meet and share God's love with, and we met a guy who was manning the AA Breakdown stand in the town centre. Even though he was very adamant about being an atheist, what stood out to us both was his compassion and faithfulness. This man was caring long term for his wife who was currently sick and waiting for a kidney donor and who had been on dialysis since she was born. We learned how he was getting up very early, doing everything for his wife and children, travelling a distance to work and then returning in the evening to do the same again, and all with apparent cheerfulness and devotion. We honoured and encouraged him for being such a good husband and father.

Some friends and I often take the opportunity to encourage the manager of the Costa we meet in. We noticed the way he related to and trained his staff and we were struck by his vision and passion, always looking for the best in his team. We decided to write a card telling him and encouraging him and he still has our card posted on his staffroom wall.

Now you could be thinking we are simply promoting people's 'good works' when Jesus said it is not by your good works that you will inherit the Kingdom of God. Not at all. Instead, I believe when we show love and honour to those who God has made we are actually helping them to connect with who He is. We are pointing them to the God who made them to live this way and who desires relationship with them.

Being motivated by love

Paul writes, *'Let all that you do be done in love'* (1 Corinthians 16:14). God will only bless what is motivated by love. As we seek to demonstrate Christ's love there will be obstacles we have to face, such as being mistreated or misunderstood. Often, though, the obstacles can actually be the motivations of our own hearts. Along the way I have experienced each of these. I have called them the three 'P's: performance, pleasing others and pride.

Performance

Performance is our attempt to impress God but it can have two outcomes. Either it can stop us evangelising because we feel a failure and end up believing it's only for special people, or we perform and do it in our own strength. We can slip into loving people because it's the Christian thing to do or because we feel pressured. I know there have been times when I've thought I was pleasing God through my acts of evangelism whilst all the time operating from a place of 'I ought to' rather than from love. This kind of motivation is rooted in performance.

I remember one time when I stepped out to pray for a lady who looked lonely. I discovered she had a hearing problem and so I offered to pray for her. She was adamant God had sent her hearing problem as well as the other health issues she had. I boldly told her that wasn't true and wanted to show her by praying for her for Jesus to heal her. After praying a couple of times and nothing changing I came away confused, disappointed and angry towards God. I didn't understand why He didn't heal this lady. Even though I still don't know why, I know it certainly wasn't because Jesus was reluctant to heal. As I spent time with God asking questions, I realised I was more concerned about my performance and the outcome than about loving this lady well.

The good news of the gospel is that it's neither about our performance or the outcome. We don't need to witness to please Jesus because He is already pleased with us. Being motivated by God's love for people and knowing we have His 'yes' means that when we step out in obedience, even in a public place with other people watching, we know the outcome is up to Him. As I've grown in my identity as a daughter and in knowing my Father's love for me, I've become far more courageous.

When we know we are His sons and daughters, it's so freeing because we know that our influence flows out of who we are and not what we do. Heidi Baker says, 'We do because we are loved – not to be loved. We do because we are accepted – not to be accepted.'[2] I love being around people who know they are loved and cherished, it shows in how they speak and what they do. There is a lightness and freedom about them that is contagious and attractive. When we live from the Father's approval it leads us to love others boldly but from a place of rest. When I hear the enemy whispering in my ear, 'You can't do this,' I tell him, 'I know I can't, but I am connected to the One who can!'

Pleasing others

Sometimes we can be motivated by a need to please others. This has been quite a journey for me as I came from a background where I felt I had to perform to be loved. Fear of letting people down or getting it wrong has often stopped me stepping forward. When we're afraid of making a mistake it stops us from stepping out and taking risks.

For some time I had been asking God for words of knowledge for people I met on the street or outside of the church. Words of knowledge are when God reveals information about someone to us that we couldn't possibly have known. It's one of the ways God shows people how much He loves them and how He knows all about them, as with the woman at the well. As I've been learning to listen and then step out with what I think God is saying, there have been times when the words have been right but plenty of times, too, when they have been wrong! In the past I would have felt such a heavy sense of shame and failure about getting it wrong and it would have stopped me stepping out again. Now I'm learning to relax and say ok, that was wrong, and I'm learning to be more relaxed, not to take myself so seriously, and to keep going. Because I know I am loved and my value is not dependent on my performance I hear the Father's encouragement, 'Go again, Claire!' When the disciples couldn't cast out the demon, Jesus didn't rebuke them; instead He saw it as a teaching and training opportunity, all the time teaching them about deeper trust and dependence.

Pride

Another motivation can be pride; wanting a good story to tell to impress others. When the seventy-two returned to Jesus full of joy after seeing many miracles through their hands, they said to Jesus, *'Even the demons are subject to us in your name!'* (Luke 10:17). They were excited, as we are when God uses us. It's tempting when we are part of something wonderful God does through us to want recognition as we tell the story. Jesus agreed that He had given them authority over all the power of the enemy but He reminded them not to rejoice in what they had done but that their names were written in heaven.

As we celebrate and share stories, which we must always keep doing, let's remember that we're not the centre of the story, Jesus is!

Our stories are His stories and everyone else's too.

Jesus' counter-cultural way of love is challenging at every level. He even reminds us not to prefer our friends' company so much that we neglect those He has called us to reach. One time I had a dream where I had invited all my close friends to spend the evening with me, friends who I love to be with. In my dream I noticed others had come too and they were drug addicts, prostitutes and people I wouldn't have chosen to invite, even people I considered intimidating. Then in the dream I saw myself praying for them to receive the Holy Spirit and one by one they were falling under the power of the Spirit. This dream provokes me that God has called me out of what is safe and predictable to live a radical lifestyle of love and power. Jesus said, *'When you give a dinner or a banquet, do not invite your friends or your brothers or your relatives or rich neighbours, lest they also invite you in return and you be repaid. But when you give a feast, invite the poor, the crippled, the lame, the blind, and you will be blessed, because they cannot repay you'* (Luke 14:12-14). As I write this and remember that dream I feel freshly provoked.

Loving like Jesus is sacrificial and costly and requires us to step beyond where we feel comfortable, to stop when we'd rather walk on by.

> **Love isn't always convenient and often leads us into situations that are messy.**

Ed Stetzer says, 'The Christian life is not about safety and comfort, but rather about finding yourself in a dangerous place of vulnerable compassion.'[3] In our culture of comfort it is so easy for us to anaesthetise ourselves but in order to engage with compassion we need to be willing to connect with people's pain. This is both exciting and scary. I am so aware of my weaknesses but when I step out trusting in God's love working through me, I am amazed at the wonderful things I see happen.

As we keep saying yes to Him and step out with courage to love this way, God grows in us the ability to love the people He puts in front of us. Although it is sometimes painful, it is the Father's love to strip away all that we depend on so that He alone is the One we trust. I am so grateful God doesn't wait for us to be perfected in love before He moves through us but instead He makes us more like Him on the journey. He is most glorified in our weakness.

Growing in compassion

We see in the gospels how Jesus regularly withdrew to a quiet place to pray and His ministry always flowed from a place of humility and rest. This was the rhythm of Jesus' life on earth. Even after Jesus had just angrily overturned the tables in the temple, He then healed the blind and the lame. I've often wondered how He could move from anger to compassion so quickly. He was righteously and deeply angry and yet He was also full of compassion and mercy. We see the same when He healed the man with the withered hand. Even in the face of shouts of indignation He proclaimed truth that challenged people to the core. Because He was secure in His identity and He only ever did what His Father showed Him, He was peacefully poised.

I am learning that the more time I spend with the Father experiencing His love and compassion for me, the more I am growing in compassion for others. His love is unconditional and unceasing. We cannot earn it and there is nothing we can ever do to stop God loving us this way.

> The more our hearts are connected with His love, the more His love moves us to act and show compassion for others. We really can only give away what we have first received.

Love always looks like something

Every day we have an opportunity to give away and to show love and, as you'll see through some of the stories in this book, it can look like many things. Love may be praying for someone and telling them about Jesus but it may sometimes be simply offering to buy someone a coffee just to bless them. Love might look like offering to pay for someone's groceries in the supermarket or offering to take someone's dog for a walk. So many times I have seen how a timely act of kindness and generosity – whether a coffee, a bunch of flowers, a text of encouragement or a tray of cakes – has brought hope to someone in the midst of a difficult day or a challenging season. Love may look like thanking people who are doing very menial jobs like cleaning toilets or the streets or thanking traffic wardens who often receive abuse rather than appreciation.

As a result of a prophetic word given to King's Arms Church God spoke to one of our leaders about initiating something called a 'Tsunami of Love'. He said, 'Imagine hundreds and even thousands of acts of love and kindness being poured out through you and me. Spontaneous or planned, sometimes practical, always unconditional, generous and unexpected being passed on to others, with the simple invitation to pass on the kindness to someone else.' The invitation to pass it on comes through a little token, like a small coin, which we can slip in with our gift. On the token there is a website address where people can read stories and find out more about Jesus (tsunamioflove.co.uk). Within a year of starting there were just over 500 recorded acts of kindness with many follow-up stories. This isn't a gimmick; it is a response of love, the love we have come to know that is the foundation of our life in Christ.

However we do good to someone, whether it's buying a drink for them or praying for their healing, we are demonstrating the Kingdom. As we give generously, show acceptance without judgment and display kindness and mercy, we show people something of who the Father is and what He is like. As we give humbly expecting nothing in return, we are being Jesus to people. This is being moved by love and His love is so extravagant, generous and full of kindness that it's a beautiful thing when we see His Kingdom break out. Sometimes even miracles happen!

CHAPTER SIX

Step Into My Shoes

**My sheep hear my voice, and I know them,
and they follow me.**

John 10:27

A few years ago in a time of worship I heard the Father say, 'Step into My shoes.' That was it. It was so brief and yet so clear to me that I replied, 'How can I do that? 'You are God!' As I was pondering what I had just heard, I had a picture come into my mind of a child trying to walk in big shoes just like one of my granddaughters who used to love clip-clopping around in my heels. Thinking about how children love to copy and try on shoes that are too big for them, I sensed the Father saying, 'I'm inviting you to do the same. I want you to imitate Me, to follow Me and to go where I lead you into things that are too big for you.' It was such a precious moment of encounter. Later I was reminded that shoes represent the gospel and I felt a skip in my heart because I knew the Father was leading me somewhere I hadn't been before. I knew God was inviting me into a greater place of intimacy with Him.

It brings our Father delight when we dare to trust Him for things too big for us, the greater things He has promised we will do. So often we limit ourselves to what fits and what we are familiar with. It takes a child to show us the fun of faith and to believe that we can! I knew it was the Father speaking to me because it didn't feel heavy or hard, it felt light, easy and fun and I wanted to go there. As I write this, God has reminded me of when I was a child and learning to swim.

Those who couldn't swim wore red swimming caps and those who could wore white ones. I was 'a red cap' and had been for some considerable time. I longed to wear a white cap and one day I told the teacher of the white-cap swimmers I believed I could now swim, and she let me have a go. I remember thinking something magical would happen when I jumped into the deep water and that it would somehow hold me up, but to my surprise if didn't and I went down and down until the teacher hauled me up. I then, of course, got sent back to the red caps. Even though this story reminds me of the need to persevere to reach the goal (I did eventually learn to swim!), it also reminds me that children don't place limits on their imagination. As someone once said, 'Children always believe that something wonderful is about to happen.'

A week after this encounter with God, I went to the hairdressers as usual. Mine is a 'walk in' one and there was quite a long wait. I sat between two women, thinking about this invitation from the Father, and I asked the Holy Spirit what He was doing and how I could join in. I wondered which of the women He might like me to speak to. I felt drawn to the lady on my left and even though she was playing a game on her phone, she seemed happy to stop and chat. After some initial small talk, Rachel began telling me enthusiastically about her work in healthcare. She seemed very grateful to have her job and I sensed that life previously hadn't been easy for her.

As we talked on Rachel opened up and told me how in the past she'd been homeless and a resident at the King's Arms Project.[1] When she heard I was part of the King's Arms church her face lit up. She was remembering someone who had been very kind to her there and kept asking if I knew of them. Philippa, a long-standing member of our King's Arms Project, of which the night shelter is a vital part, had clearly had a big impact on her. As Rachel was recalling this time in her life she kept adding, 'I'm not religious though.' I told her, 'And neither am I, but I love Jesus and He has completely changed my life.'

She looked surprised by my reply and asked when that was. I told her that it began forty plus years ago and I would have told her my story but at that moment she got called to have her hair cut. As I sat reflecting on our conversation the Holy Spirit spoke to me and said that I had been another reminder of the Father's goodness and kindness in Rachel's life, pointing her to Him. She had clearly not forgotten Philippa from our church who had helped her, been kind to her and left a deposit in her life.

Over the next few months God kept highlighting to me how many people I meet who don't yet know Jesus, and yet have had some kind of a 'spiritual' experience, one which they've never forgotten. Perhaps you've noticed the same.

I remember once talking to a butcher in our town and as soon as I mentioned God in our conversation he told me of a time he had been in a field alone and felt a hand on his shoulder. He said he'd never forgotten it. Another lady told me how she had been on a family walk. As she'd separated and walked at a distance she said she'd felt a presence she couldn't explain but which she knew was good because she hadn't felt afraid. I'm reminded, too, of a friend of mine who met a man in our town. During their conversation the man told my friend that he'd had a dream he'd never been able to forget. In the dream he had seen a book open with lots of names in it and when he'd looked his name wasn't there. He asked my friend what he thought it meant. After sharing the gospel with the man, my friend got to then lead him in a prayer to receive Jesus.

As I asked God why He kept highlighting these stories to me I felt Him say, 'I want you to remind My people that wherever they go and wherever they sow seed, they leave a deposit of My love in people's lives. They are like spiritual markers pointing people to Me.' We know God reveals Himself to people in so many wonderful ways. I have heard many stories of people who have encountered God coming to them in a vision or dream or simply through creation. People have met with God as they opened up the Bible and as they heard the gospel preached to them. Whatever way God gets people's attention it is always to reveal His great love.

> **God is giving us the privilege of being Daniels and Josephs in our generation: translating God to the people we meet, helping to interpret their dreams or their spiritual experiences and pointing them to Jesus.**

I met a pastor, Mark, who told me this story. He was driving west out of Cambridge and, from nowhere, felt a strong impetus to turn around. He felt God prompt him to drive all the way across the city and have a coffee in Starbucks, on the east side of the city. Having got there, Mark sat drinking his coffee, feeling that it was all a bit stupid if he had got it wrong. Just at that moment a young lady arrived carrying a copy of *Piercing the Darkness*, a novel written some years ago.[2] He started to talk about the book with her and discovered that she had grown up around church but had lost her faith and was very disillusioned. Someone from her family had lent her the book and she said she was thinking about reading it. Mark was able to share a few things with her and encourage her to read the book and ask questions. She had only planned to be in Cambridge for an hour and was in Starbucks to pass the time before picking someone up and driving back home, some 60 miles away.

Mark told me that a year later he received a text out of the blue, which said, 'Not sure if you will remember me but we met in Starbucks in Cambridge about a year ago. I was reading *Piercing the Darkness* and we got chatting. We spoke about church and God and you left me your card. Well I had lost the card but was praying last night and thought to open the same book that I was reading as it's helped me immensely and your card fell out! Just to let you know I am now leading the youth department in our church and I would love to catch up and connect again with you guys.' Mark, who leads a church in Cambridge, said, 'I was really encouraged by this; it's always worth taking a risk and following God. We will only occasionally see the results of what we sow – but seeing that God will use what we sow, let's sow faithfully, genuinely and from love and He will give the increase.'

Imagine, wherever we go, being led by the Holy Spirit this way. When the Spirit spoke to Philip and led him to the Ethiopian eunuch, He placed Philip beside the chariot at just the right time. It was clear by his spiritual thirst that God was already at work in this man's life but it was Philip's readiness to listen and his obedience to go that led him to partner with what God was already doing.

When God spoke to Ananias and told him to go and pray for Saul, he knew God was telling him to go to a man who had made murderous threats to Christians. He knew that it was at the risk of his own life, yet he went, and his courageous act of obedience was an important part of Paul becoming one of the most significant leaders of the church.

When Peter received a vision that was contrary to his experience and way of thinking as a Jew about what was clean and unclean he could have dismissed it. Instead, because he knew it was God speaking to him, he got up and obeyed and the vision led him to the house of Cornelius. As a result, Cornelius and his whole household came to Christ and it was the beginning of the gospel being preached to the Gentiles and the rest of the world.

Even when it doesn't seem to make sense to us, the more we follow where the Spirit leads the more we will see the beauty of what He is doing.

My friend Sue was relaxing at home alone one Sunday afternoon when she had a strong sense from God that there was a young woman coming by train for an abortion and that God wanted her to go and meet her. When her husband returned from the park with their three young children, she told him and, being the man of God he is, he encouraged her to go. 'But,' she argued, 'that was a while ago and how did God know what time you'd come back? And what if I drive the five miles to the station too slowly or too fast? I'll miss her!' Her husband replied, 'If God said go to the station, go!'

As Sue neared the station, she saw a couple walking up the hill carrying a small red suitcase and knew this was who God had told her about. She followed discreetly in the car to see if they were in fact headed for the abortion clinic – and they of course were. As my friend parked the car, she saw they were sitting on the step by the front door waiting for the clinic to open for the evening admissions. Unknown to my friend, the abortion clinic admitted women on a Sunday evening who were booked in for a late termination the following day. Not knowing quite what she was going to say, she approached them and explained that God had spoken to her that afternoon. That He cared so much about them and their circumstances that He would send her to tell them that He loved them and that there was another way. The man told Sue that they hadn't taken the decision lightly. Even though the girl didn't say anything her response was emotional and she welled up. After leaving them Sue prayed and has never forgotten the girl with the red hair and bright red suitcase.

As a result of this encounter, Sue said she never wanted a woman with an unplanned pregnancy to have to say 'Where was God when I needed Him?' A counselling service, run by a group of churches, was born out of this encounter nearly 30 years ago and is still helping women today. Since then, hundreds and possibly thousands of women have been given the space to think about their situation and to consider the options open to them. My friend says mostly they have not known the outcome, but some have returned to tell their story. As a result of this service there may be many women who have gone on to keep their babies and some finding faith in God in the process. This all came from listening to God and stepping out in obedience, even when it made no 'earthly' sense.

Learning to follow

I have always been interested in what other people are doing, some would say nosy! As a child, if we were taken out to a restaurant I remember my dad would make sure he sat me where I could see everyone so I didn't turn around and stare. Some years ago, in a time of waiting on God, I asked Him to show me what He sees when He thinks of me. Straight into my mind came the word 'espionage'. It wasn't at all what I was expecting! As I lay on the floor God reminded me of Joshua and Caleb who spied out the land and brought back a good report and I felt stirred and excited to be on a similar mission. I believe this is for all of us. God invites us to go where He leads, to see with eyes of faith and, just like Joshua and Caleb, to encourage others to do the same.

Learning to follow means staying attentive. As God is taking me on this journey I'm noticing how the Holy Spirit sometimes gets my attention not because He wants me to do or say anything but just simply to watch what He's doing. I love these moments of intimacy with Him.

One time a family group were walking towards us in the park, chatting and enjoying their takeaway coffees. A little girl amongst them suddenly came running up to me to show me her hot chocolate. She was just so delighted with it. I didn't know this family or this little girl but in that moment I sensed the Father showing me how much He delighted over her enjoyment.

Another time I saw an elderly couple on a bench who looked very sad and tired. There was a group of small children who were having such fun throwing armfuls of leaves up into the air in front of them. Sadly their mums stopped them as though they should have known not to play with the leaves. What the Father showed me in that moment was how much He loved it and how their childlike joy was for this couple to enjoy. Children seem to beautifully express wonder in the present moment and find joy in the smallest of things; things as adults we can often miss.

As I am learning to follow, I am becoming far more attentive to what is happening around me. I'm also realising how much fun it is learning to live this way. It is the Holy Spirit who sets up the situations and it's He who opens people's hearts; we just have to say yes and follow Him into them. It is always His work, which means that the pressure is off. Even though our yes may seem a small response in the moment, it is often part of something much bigger that God is about. The following story is one such example.

One time when I was walking through Bedford Park with my friend Jules we passed a young woman on a bench. Even though it's quite normal to see someone sitting alone in a park, for some reason, as I passed by, I sensed a feeling of sadness around her. I felt drawn but I continued to walk on, as I needed to get home. Jules picked up on what I was sensing and encouraged me to go back, which I did. Approaching the lady I said I was sorry to disturb her but wondered if she was ok, as I'd noticed she looked sad. She straightaway started to cry and with gentle questions we found out she had lost a lot of people very close to her in a short space of time. She was grief-stricken; she was not sleeping and was very depressed. The girl told us how she had set out to do some Christmas shopping but hadn't been able to face the crowds and had come to the park looking for some peace. As we listened and showed love to this girl, who was called Sally, we spoke words of hope over her. She told us she was a Christian but had stopped going to church because she had felt she was being such a burden to them. This meeting would have been remarkable enough but then something else extraordinary happened. As we were still talking to Sally another lady walked past, stopped and said, 'And I feel the same.' Literally they were her first words to us! She went on to tell us how she had been walking up and down the park looking for hope and then, feeling embarrassed, she started to cry.

Now two women, one who was looking for peace and the other who was looking for hope, were sitting with us as we all squashed together on the bench. My friend and I stared at each other; we could hardly believe what was happening. As we reached out to hold the hand of this second lady, called Jennifer, she told us she had been crying and was very fearful. She'd had a scan on her shoulder the previous day for an ongoing problem that wasn't responding to treatment and she was clearly worried about the outcome. We offered to pray for her shoulder and as soon as Jules prayed all the pain instantly left and Jennifer was able to raise her arm above her head. She was very surprised and said that not only had the pain left but that she felt different inside.

As we prayed I asking God what He wanted to say to these ladies and I saw a picture of a lighted candle in both their hearts. What I saw were two tea lights and then, immediately after, Isaiah 42:3 came to mind: *'A bruised reed he will not break, and a faintly burning wick he will not quench; he will faithfully bring forth justice.'* As I prayed it over them I felt God's compassion and His tenderness towards them. Jennifer, also a Christian, was now encouraging Sally and we told them that maybe they should connect and encourage each other. Sadly, despite following up with Sally we had no further contact, but Jennifer continued to stay in touch and visited our church one Sunday and came to find me.

Growing into childlike faith

Stepping into His shoes requires bold, childlike faith and as sons and daughters this is God's design for us. There is something about becoming like a child that clearly invites the Holy Spirit. Children don't complicate things in the way we often do. I love this story a father in our church told me.

A few Saturdays ago, when my wife Sarah was out for the day, I was looking after the children and having lunch. Livvy, my six-year old daughter, was asking questions about the baby in mummy's tummy and asked if I knew the name of the baby! I deflected the question by telling her how God knows everything about the baby and is 'knitting him together'. She responded, 'Great, so let's ask God what his name is!' She instructed everyone to close their eyes and proceeded by asking, 'Please, God, tell us the baby's name.' She paused and then asked if we heard anything. I scrambled to think how I should handle this, whether it should be an explanation of how we hear from God or something similar. Quick as a flash she said, 'Right, let's try again then.' I can't take any credit for her persistence; she has obviously seen this modelled elsewhere! She asked if we had heard anything, to which I again replied no and she tried again! This time, she then said, 'I think God said the baby's name is William.' To my complete surprise, it was the name Sarah and I had been discussing and were settling on!

Just like that little girl, I think God wants us to be like children who take Him at His word, delighting in who He is and boldly stepping out in faith. The book of Acts is full of stories of the church living this way.

> **There is something about staying close and being hungry for God that seems to lead us to step into more than we've yet seen.**

The more we wonder at who He is, the bigger our view of God, and the more dependent we are the more we will trust God for the seemingly impossible. This is a story of just that.

Eight years ago Lizzie, a friend of ours who was already suffering with depression, was diagnosed with Stage 4 oesophageal cancer. The hospital said they couldn't do anything more for her and that she should put things in order and not expect to live many more months. It was a terrible shock for everyone. A friend of mine gathered a few of us to pray and over the period of about a year we met regularly to worship and pray with Lizzie for a miracle.

God spoke to us in many ways during that time. He spoke about having faith the size of a mustard seed and how we could speak to the mountain of cancer and tell it to move, which we did on many occasions. God even sent a man from New Zealand, who himself had been healed of terminal cancer, to pray for our friend. Lizzie's sister Jane had remembered hearing Craig Marsh, a visiting pastor from New Zealand, speak about his miraculous healing from stomach cancer at an event in West Sussex two years previously and told Lizzie about it.

As Lizzie watched Craig's story on YouTube she identified with him as he related his experiences and God planted a seed of faith in Lizzie's heart to believe for a miracle. Lizzie writes in her book *Swallowed by Life* how she said to herself, 'If God can heal Craig, why can't He heal me?' This was a turning point for Lizzie and she emailed Craig asking him to pray for her. Much to her surprise Craig replied by return saying that he and the church in Sydney, where he was ministering at the time, would pray for her. Lizzie discovered how miraculous that reply was because, as he later told her, he receives up to ninety emails a day and had not time to read them all. Craig had opened his laptop that day and, glancing over dozens of emails, one had caught his attention, the subject line: Prayer Request for Healing of Oesophageal Cancer, which was from Lizzie.

It was some time before she heard from Craig again but months later she had the news that he was coming to the UK and Lizzie could hardly believe he was coming half way around the world just for her. As a prayer group our eyes were on God but our faith was definitely stirred by his visit, in fact we became Craig's ministry team as he both prayed for Lizzie and as he ministered at local churches during his stay.

On the first occasion Craig prayed for Lizzie he anointed her forehead with oil before he and we gently laid hands on her and prayed for her healing. Craig kept reminding us that he couldn't heal anyone; that it was God's remit. Lizzie writes, 'We knew God was there with us, He was almost touchable and we sensed that anything could happen!'

Lizzie was very tired and went to lie down on her bed for a rest. From that time onwards she says she never needed a daytime rest. Her sister Sue who was a nurse observed also that her countenance that had previously been quite grey was now pink and she wasn't as breathless as previously. Craig prayed for Lizzie four more times and then said, 'I don't think we need to pray for you again.' This marked the early stages of what we came to see as a beautiful healing in process.

Through it all God led us to keep worshipping and to fix our eyes on Him. We regularly emailed or texted Lizzie both words we felt God give us, plus our joy and delight at all He was doing. None of us had walked this way before or seen such a miracle but over the course of a year we watched our friend get better and better until the hospital confirmed that there was no cancer left in her body. Even the metal stent they had fitted had miraculously disappeared. I remember the evening when I was driving to her house to pray and I felt the Holy Spirit say, 'It's done.' It was a short time after that we saw the miracle we, and many others, had been contending for. We were ecstatic. I often look back and remember how childlike our faith was and how we were just a bunch of hungry women pressing into God for more.

Hebrews 11 reminds us that faith is the expectation of things not yet seen and lists many heroes who demonstrated such faith: men and women who believed that nothing was impossible for God. I wonder, how do we keep on living with the same courage and expectation? I will talk about courage in the next chapter but I am provoked by their example. I believe that the hungrier we are for God's presence the more of His Kingdom and the miraculous we will see breaking out around us. As Bill Johnson says, 'Bold faith stands on the shoulders of quiet trust.'[3]

Learning to recognise the nudges of the Holy Spirit

When we are intentional about looking for opportunities to bring God's Kingdom the Holy Spirit always seems to draw close. I am very much on a journey in all of this but I'd love to pass on some of the ways I've noticed the Holy Spirit getting my attention. These are not formulas. Walking with the Holy Spirit is beautifully mysterious. Generally, though, I have noticed that either the Holy Spirit leads us to people or He leads people to us. Some of the ways I have recognised the latter have been when people have suddenly started talking to me or telling me what's wrong with them.

One time I was sitting in a café reading and having a coffee before a hair appointment. I looked up and noticed a lady about to sit down at a nearby table trying to juggle her coffee and a walking stick. I smiled at her sympathetically and asked if she was ok. She sighed and said to me, 'Peace at last! It's my only day to myself. I care fulltime for my mother who has dementia, I recently lost my mother-in-law and I have just come from bereavement counselling.' Recognising the Holy Spirit's invitation I listened and then invited this lady, who was called Lynn, to come and sit with me. She was beginning to share personal information and I wanted her to feel safe. Lynn was happy to join me and for the next two hours I listened as she shared about some of the pain, losses and disappointments in her life. When she asked about me I shared a little of my story and I got to talk about Jesus and to share the gospel with her. She listened intently and said it reminded her of a time she had gone into an abbey and felt something very strongly that had made her cry. Lynn asked me what I thought it was and I asked her what she thought it was. She said she thought it was the presence of God, and I agreed. I told her that it was God drawing her because He knew her and loved her and that He wanted to have relationship with her. She began to cry and I asked if I could pray for her that she would know God personally, and she allowed me to pray for her. She seemed really impacted by our meeting and at the end she said, 'I wasn't going to come in here today; I don't like going into places on my own, but then you started talking to me.'

Another way I notice the Holy Spirit getting my attention is when I feel compassion for someone. Sometimes it seems obvious because I can see someone is in pain or has a need, but other times I don't know why God is highlighting them until I take a risk and step out and speak to them. When I feel compassion for someone who I can see is in pain I usually approach them and ask them what's going on. I often say, 'Hi, how are you doing? Are you in pain? I see you have to use crutches.' I find that people are usually more than happy to talk about what's going on for them or to tell you their story.

One time we saw a man with crutches limping as he came into the coffee shop where we hold our prayer café. I went across to the man who was sitting with a little boy at a table nearby. We had noticed the boy had been looking at our banner and trying to get his uncle's attention because he knew it said something about healing. The man was polite but shy whilst his little nephew was very eager and emotional as he told me what had happened to his uncle.

Havira was visiting from Spain and had tripped whilst getting off a Tube train in London. I asked Havira if he'd like me to pray for his ankle and shyly he thanked me saying that he was ok. I could see the disappointment on his nephew's face and I was moved by this little boy's compassion and desire for his uncle to be healed. I always love to tell people what Jesus has already done and so told them both the story of a lady whose ankle had been healed just a few weeks before in the same café. The little boy and I were so glad when I offered again to pray and Havira said, 'Go on, why not?'

I bent down and laid my hands on Havira's ankle and prayed for Jesus to heal and restore it. After testing it out Havira said there was some improvement and he was so touched, he said he wanted to thank God. Closing his eyes he bowed his head and then prayed a beautiful heartfelt prayer of thanksgiving. Wow! I knew God wanted to do more and so I asked him if I could pray again. He agreed and testing it out afterwards he found he was able to move and bend his ankle freely which he said he hadn't been able to do before. Havira was delighted, as was his nephew. I asked if he knew Jesus who had just healed him and he told me he knew about Jesus, had been raised a Catholic but had not been to church for a long time. We had a very warm conversation about knowing Jesus personally and I then left him to enjoy his family time and coffee.

A few minutes later I looked up and saw shy Havira boldly walking up and down the café testing out his healed ankle. Before leaving he allowed us to video his story of healing, which is posted on our Facebook page (costahealingcafebedford). As he left carrying his crutches, he told us he was excited to tell his sister, who is a Christian, what God had done for him that day.

Treasure hunting

Knowing people are God's treasure and that He has sent us to tell them, we sometimes use a tool called 'treasure hunting'. Treasure hunting is simply asking God for clues – i.e. words of knowledge – that lead us to people He wants us to meet. It involves asking God for the name of someone, where you will meet them, and something that describes their appearance as well as something that might be wrong with them. I have heard of so many wonderful stories as people have gone treasure hunting with the Holy Spirit. I still remember my first experience.

We had been given just three minutes to wait on God asking Him for clues. The reason for a short time, I later discovered, is that God really doesn't need a long time to speak to us, plus we can so easily over analyse what we think God has said. I was convinced, however, that I had probably made up some of the clues I had written on my piece of paper. They were 'Sam', 'garage' and 'overalls.' Our son is called Sam and at the time was a mechanic in the Royal Marines so you can see where I was going with this. Our group had various other clues, two of which were 'someone tall' and 'someone with a bad back'. Armed with our clues the plan was to go out and look for the treasure – the people who matched our clues, who God wanted us to speak to.

Our small group of four set off locally and our team leader felt we should head for the car showroom nearby, as that seemed the closest to my location clue, 'garage'. As we walked up the path to the showroom the only person in sight was a man up a ladder. I know we were all feeling pretty terrified. Whether I just wasn't showing my fear or not, I don't know, but our team leader encouraged me to go first. I awkwardly called up to the person on the ladder and said, 'Excuse me, sorry to disturb you but we are doing an alternative treasure hunt and we have some clues we would like to show you to see if they mean anything to you.'

The man was very friendly and came down the ladder and looked at our list of clues. None of them meant anything to him and though disappointed we thanked him and were about to leave. Suddenly, with a small ounce of courage, I asked him if he happened to know anyone called Sam who worked in a garage and was wearing overalls. He said straightaway, 'Oh yes, Sam, he works in the garage round the back!' I couldn't believe it! I hadn't made it up; God really had spoken to me! As two of us went round the back, sure enough we discovered a large garage. We asked for Sam who we found bent over the bonnet of a car. Not only was he very tall but he also suffered with a bad back. We had the opportunity to pray for Sam's back and tell him how God had led us to him. I'm not sure who was more surprised!

Again, I think children and young people can teach us so much. They are quicker to receive and not filter the things God shows them. In Bob Johnson's book *Love Stains* I love this story he tells about his son, as they set out on a similar treasure hunt.

'Ok, son, what are you going to bring?' I looked down at Nash, my ten-year-old son. His big eyes, keenly observant as usual, sparkled back at me. 'Bungee cords,' he answered. Bungee cords. I nodded, knowing that Nash was one of the most sensitive people I'd ever known. If he heard 'bungee cords', he heard 'bungee cords'. I would always tell my team to ask the Holy Spirit if they should bring, purchase or do something for that special 'one' the Lord was sending them to that night before we would go out. The Lord often uses a simple gift, action or word to break open the hardest walls and heal the most wounded hearts. We are always looking for the 'one' and we are always asking the Lord what we can give or do or say to find the treasure in that one. We went to a hardware store and picked up a set of brand-new bungee cords and soon we were on the streets looking for the person God wanted us to find that night and give bungee cords to. Several hours passed before Nash pointed her out to me. An old woman pushing a dilapidated stand-up cart piled high with boxes. Nash nudged me, 'Dad,' he motioned with his eyes. 'She needs bungee cords.' I watched from a distance as my son made his way up to the old woman. I heard him say faintly, looking into her eyes, 'Ma'am? God told me to give these bungee cords to you.' He handed her the cords and she started to cry as I watched, the invisible witness from the sidelines. Those bungee cords had stirred up something deep in her spirit. I couldn't hear what was said next, but I saw my son lay his hands on her and pray for her, tears streaming down her face. He wrapped his hands around her and hugged her like he would his grandmother. She hugged him just as hard back, and then she slipped off into the night pushing her cart and boxes now securely fastened with bungee cords, still wiping her eyes and marvelling that God knew what she needed. It was a divine appointment with bungee cords . . . Divine appointments like that serve as a sort of heavenly bridge

between the Holy Spirit and the one God has His eye on. When we are obedient to do exactly what God says (like bringing bungee cords along on a walk through the streets) God will move. Obedience and 'ears to hear' pave the way for a real God encounter unlike any memorised five-step one-phrase-fits-all ever could.[4]

I recently heard a story from a mum about her son who had attended Newday a couple of years ago. Newday is a large Christian 'youth' event that takes place in the UK every year. As well as worship and teaching, the young people have the opportunity to practically serve the local community and, as part of this, treasure hunting is one of the outreach activities they are introduced to. After spending a short time in prayer asking God for clues, this young boy had a clear picture of a front door, the house number and a pair of wellington boots outside the door. This was his first experience of treasure hunting with God. As they went out he kept looking for this house that he had seen in his mind and eventually they came across it. Not only was the house number correct but also there was a pair of wellington boots outside. He wrote a note of encouragement he felt God give to him and posted it through the letterbox.

Some time later the next-door neighbours got to hear about it and got in touch. It turned out that they were Christians and had been praying for the family living in the house with the wellington boots outside! God was clearly pursuing this family.

We know God can get people's attention in a myriad of ways without any help from us, yet He chooses to invite us to partner with Him. Living this way is both scary and fun. I have found that learning to step into His shoes that are too big for me always requires taking a risk. You have to take risks to see God's Kingdom advance. For example, you cannot know if a word of knowledge is right unless you share it. You cannot know if someone will get healed unless you pray. You cannot know if someone is ready to give their life to Jesus unless you ask them the question. Having to take risks forces us to be continually dependent on God, which deepens our relationship with Him. It reminds us of our weakness and His strength and it ensures that God gets all the glory when His Kingdom advances through us.

Living a naturally supernatural life is not comfortable but it's the adventurous lifestyle we are all called to live. Because Jesus lives inside of us we get to work alongside Him. This is prophetic evangelism, learning to partner with heaven as we show people who the Father is and what He is like. Every day as we receive the love of the Father and look to give it away we become imitators of Christ and step into His shoes.

CHAPTER SEVEN

A People of Courage

'For truly, I say to you, if you have faith like a grain of mustard seed, you will say to this mountain, "Move from here to there", and it will move, and nothing will be impossible for you.'

Matthew 17:20

It was the last supper and Jesus was preparing His disciples for His departure. He knew both their sadness and the temptations they would face to disperse and lose heart. He told them, *'Abide in me, and I in you. As the branch cannot bear fruit by itself, unless it abides in the vine, neither can you, unless you abide in me. I am the vine; you are the branches. Whoever abides in me and I in him, he it is that bears much fruit, for apart from me you can do nothing'* (John 15:4-5).

Here Jesus was speaking of our union with Him where He abides in us and we abide in Him; He was telling His friends to stay close and not shrink back. He was reminding them, too, of their identity and purpose. Jesus said, *'You did not choose me, but I chose you and appointed you that you should go and bear fruit and that your fruit should abide'* (John 15:16). Courage to be all God has called us to be flows out of our dependency on Him and walking closely with Jesus, for apart from Him we can do nothing!

In John 5:19-20 we see Jesus describing His relationship with the Father. He says, *'The Son can do nothing of Himself, but what He sees the Father do; for whatever He does the*

Son also does in like manner. For the Father loves the Son, and shows Him all things that He Himself does' (NKJV). Jesus was explaining that He did nothing independently. He was fully submitted to the Father's will. His submission came by choice and not by coercion or from a place of inferiority. It came from a place of delighting in the Father's pleasure and of the Father delighting to show the Son what He was doing.

In the same way, as we His sons and daughters delight in the Father's pleasure, He delights to show us what He is doing and invites us to join in. Encountering intimacy with the Father in this way leads us to act boldly and courageously from our true identity. Everything flows from this place of rest, of us knowing who God is and believing who He says we are.

Most Christians I speak to want to be more courageous both in telling others about Jesus and offering to pray for the sick, and Jesus wants this too! Just like the disciples, though, we are all on a journey of learning to live this way. There are no super Christians or special healers; you and I are they. As Jesus prepared to send out the disciples He said, *'As the Father has sent me, even so I am sending you'* (John 20:20).

John writes in 1 John 4:17, *'As he is so also are we in this world.'* We are His hands and feet; we are His message of love.

I've often wondered what made the disciples so bold as to do the things they did, given that they were ordinary people like us. It certainly wasn't because of their credentials or qualifications. Jesus' first followers were fishermen and tax collectors and there was a zealot, a thief and a prostitute amongst them. It wasn't because they were naturally bold either, some had hidden when Jesus was being tried and then crucified. We can see in the gospels how they had the same fears and flaws as we do and yet these ordinary men and women had turned into a group who fearlessly proclaimed the resurrection. They were courageous not because of their knowledge, profile or position but because being with Jesus had changed them. Having left everything and fully surrendering their lives to Him, now full of the Spirit they had become fearless faith-filled men and women. Their courage and boldness are so provoking. Some of the apostles were beaten, shipwrecked and imprisoned for their faith. They experienced rejection, hardships and hunger yet, despite persecution, they continued to preach the gospel.

Their courage drew people's attention. When people saw the boldness of Peter and John who healed the lame man at the temple they were astounded. They knew these men were ordinary and uneducated and commented that they must have been with Jesus. After Paul and Silas preached the gospel in Thessalonica and men and women began to follow Jesus, it was said of them, *'These men who have turned the world upside down have come here also'* (Acts 17:6). Their boldness and courage came from their dependence and from their close relationship with Jesus. Filled with the Spirit the disciples knew they were sent and the book of Acts is full of stories of their obedience and courage to love.

When I think of a story that describes intimacy and courage I think of Peter stepping out of the boat and walking on water. Scripture doesn't tell us what actually motivated Peter to step out. The disciples thought they were seeing a ghost but Peter's desire was to be where Jesus was. He said, *'Lord, if it is you, command me to come to you on the water'* (Matthew 14:28). In the face of danger Jesus was exactly where he most wanted to be. He believed if Jesus called him to come it was possible, even if it meant walking on water. Peter had seen many miraculous signs performed by Jesus and he was willing to step through fear in order to be close to Him. Even though Peter did waver in his faith, stepping out of the boat was an awesome act of courage. What a hero! In the middle of the night, in the midst of a perilous storm, Peter stepped away from his only means of protection, a storm-tossed boat. In raw dependence and faith Peter fixed his eyes wholeheartedly upon Jesus with no back-up plan. It is clear from Jesus' response that even though Peter nearly sank, Jesus fully approved of Peter's faith.

Our faith brings God pleasure

The Bible says in Hebrews 11:6, *'Without faith it's impossible to please [God].'* Our trust demonstrates our wholehearted belief in God and who He is. We know that it was through faith and obedience that Noah built the ark, Abraham went to a place he didn't know, Joshua and his men marched around Jericho, and Rahab hid the spies. There are many more stories of men and women in the Bible who demonstrated great faith and obedience. I love reading stories of modern-day heroes too. People like Jackie Pullinger,[1] Brother Yun,[2] Heidi Baker, Tracy Evans,[3] and many healing evangelists down through the ages who have believed God for the impossible.

Jesus clearly celebrated people's faith. He said of the Roman centurion, who was willing to take Jesus at His word, that He had not seen such great faith before in Israel. The woman with the issue of blood as she desperately pressed through the crowds to try and touch Jesus was a courageous risk taker. Jesus told her, *'Your faith has made you well; go in peace'* (Mark 5:34). The men who broke through the roof to bring their friend to be healed by Jesus demonstrated such love and courage. Jesus said also of Mary who courageously poured expensive perfume on His feet in the face of the Pharisees' disapproval, that her act of sacrificial love and devotion would always be remembered.

Jesus showed disappointment at people's lack of faith too. In His hometown it says He could do few miracles because of their unbelief. When the storm arose and the disciples feared they would all drown He said to them, *'Oh you of little faith'* (Matthew 8:26). And when the disciples couldn't heal the boy with a demon Jesus told them that it was because of their lack of faith. Jesus went on to encourage them by saying, *'For truly, I say to you, if you have faith like a grain of mustard seed, you will say to this mountain, "Move from here to there", and it will move, and nothing will be impossible for you'* (Matthew 17:20).

Faith and courage really do go hand in hand. I wonder, are we recognisable by our courage and faith? Can people say the same of us as they said of Peter and John or of the many other heroes of the faith? It is no surprise that fear taps us on the shoulder when we are about to speak to someone about Jesus or pray for them because fear is the enemy's number-one strategy. The enemy knows that without fear we would be the most secure, the boldest and the most courageous people on earth, fully free to love others.

There are plenty of times I am not courageous and even when I've felt the nudge of the Holy Spirit I know I have not always been obedient. I remember when I used to be so full of fear that I didn't even offer to pray for anyone who was sick in case it didn't go well or in case nothing happened. I didn't want to be disappointed and I didn't want the person I was praying for to be disappointed either. Even when I did begin stepping out and praying for people I still didn't ask if anything had happened. Now when I pray for people I'm eager to ask what has happened because I believe God is the healer, I know He is good and I believe He loves to heal through me. Courage and faith come from what we believe about God and who He says He is, and then acting on it. James writes, *'Faith by itself, if it does not have works, is dead'* (James 2:17).

What are the fears that keep you from stepping out? It may be the fear of not knowing what to say or how to answer people's questions, or it may be the fear of people rejecting you. Jesus told us not to be surprised when people reject us or persecute us as He experienced the same too. Instead, God wants us to know that every time we say, 'Excuse me . . .' and step through fear to start a conversation about Jesus, He is with us. He is the one who is cheering us on. His love for the person in front of us is so much bigger than our fears.

Obedience rather than success

One evening my husband and I were going to a concert at our church. We were about to turn into our church building when

I spotted a girl across the road who was holding onto some railings and looked as though she was in some pain. I wrestled with the choice of whether to respond knowing it would make us late for the concert but then had the thought: God must have meant me to see her for a reason – something I have since learned to take more notice of.

I persuaded my husband that we should cross the road to see if we could help her. It turned out she had just sprained her ankle and was in a lot of pain. We offered to drive her where she needed to go and we also offered to pray for her. She seemed embarrassed and declined both of our offers of help saying she would be ok, even though we could see she clearly wasn't. We stayed with her, trying to reassure her, and after offering a couple more times she reluctantly agreed to let us pray for her. After a short prayer she seemed surprised and said it was in fact a little better. We wanted to pray again but she seemed anxious to go on her way and, still declining a lift, we said goodbye. I then said to her, 'Your ankle will be healed as you go.' The authority of my words shocked me, as I had never said that to anyone before. We crossed the road to the church and as I turned to look back I saw her now walking normally down the road and I was immediately reminded of when Jesus told people they would be healed as they went. I felt so happy that God had pointed her out to me. I believe every opportunity God gives us to love someone is always an invitation for His Kingdom to be made known. I also believe the more we know God's love for us and for the people He's sent us to, the bolder we'll be to have a go because His perfect love replaces our fears. Growing in courage happens as we stay close to the one who says, *'Fear not, for I am with you'* (Isaiah 41:10).

Do you know that God really does care more about our obedience than the outcome? I learned this very vividly on one occasion.

My heroic failure

I had been listening to a message preached in our church, the title of which was 'Failure is an option but timidity is not'. Phil Wilthew, one of our church leaders, spoke to us about being a people of courage; about our 'yes' being bigger than our 'no'. About being willing to attempt things for God by having a go and how this is our process of growth. This message had impacted me greatly!

Two weeks later we had an evangelist visiting our church and he invited some of us to join him in the town centre. He had just finished preaching in the town square and we were about to approach people to follow up their response. To say I was pumped with excitement was an understatement. The previous day I had seen a young man give his life to Jesus and a lady who I had prayed for wanted to meet me for coffee to find out more about Jesus. I looked around and spotted a group of young teenagers who had been watching our friend's presentation of the gospel.

Normally I would find it quite intimidating approaching a group of young teens but, provoked by Phil's message on courage, I decided to approach them. I said, 'Hey, do any of you have any sickness or pain in your bodies because I believe Jesus loves you and wants to heal you.' The teenagers went quiet and then one girl said, 'Well, I was born without any arches in my feet.' Inwardly I gulped because I knew this girl needed a creative miracle. It's funny how we measure a miracle according to the size of our faith. Hiding my fear I said, 'Can I pray for your feet?' and then choosing to step out further than I had before, I added, 'Why don't you all gather around, because I believe you are about to see God do a miracle.' I bent down and prayed. Declaring God's love for her I commanded arches to form in both her feet and then asked her to check it out to see if she could feel anything different. She said no. I had just asked if I could pray again for her when all of a sudden she ran off with the whole group of teenagers giggling after her and I was left standing there feeling a little confused and rather embarrassed.

Courageous love always requires us to take a risk. Paul writes to Timothy, *'For God has not given us a spirit of fear and timidity, but of power, love, and self-discipline'* (2 Timothy 1:7 NLT). Knowing that I am His daughter and He delights in me, I was able to dust off my disappointment, to thank God for giving me courage and to go again. Just a few weeks later I actually did get to see God do a creative miracle for someone.

Scent

One afternoon Tim, a friend of mine, wanted to join me. We were both looking to love people in our town and see what God would do. As we headed off together we felt the Holy Spirit lead us to the market square. Knowing that there would be groups of young guys hanging out in the square I was glad to be with Tim. Tim is young, chilled and streetwise whilst I, a sixty-plus female, am more comfortable approaching women and people of my own age.

All was going well until Tim started joining in with skateboarders doing tricks, leaving me on my own to have conversations. Tim had already told some of the teenagers that we were offering to pray for anyone who was sick, but no one seemed in need of prayer. A guy we'd met called Rob asked me if I knew one of his friends who went to our church, and I said I did. I noticed Rob had a very large scar across his nose and asked him what had happened to him. He proceeded to tell me the gory story of how he had been attacked with a knife and had nearly lost his nose! I asked if it had left him impaired in any way and Rob told me he wasn't able to smell strong smells. I suddenly had a moment of crazy courage and asked if I could pray for him. I knew God loved Rob and believed He could heal him. 'Well you can try,' was Rob's response.

I started to think about how we could know if there was any change to Rob's sense of smell after prayer. An idea popped into my mind that we could use my perfume as a test. After explaining my idea to Rob I squirted perfume onto my scarf and asked if he could smell it. He said he couldn't but his friend could. After praying once he said he still couldn't smell it and so I asked if I could pray again. Reluctantly he agreed. As I was praying the second time he began sniffing and screwing up his face, 'I can smell it and it's really strong!' I don't know who was more surprised!

Rob said he had to go and I felt sad that he didn't want to stay around and hear more about Jesus who had clearly just done a miracle in his life. I was reminded of the ten lepers where only one came back to thank Jesus for healing him. Whatever the outcome, I believe when we're willing to take a risk and step out of our comfort zone to love someone the way Jesus does, nothing is impossible with Him. The question needs to be not 'how big is our faith?' but 'how big is our God?' I think God wants us to be people who always live with an expectation for more than we've yet seen. The heroes of the faith we read of in scripture and down to the present day were all people who stepped out in faith because they had a big view of God.

I wonder what the church would look like if we were a people of courage, full of faith and free from fear. God spoke this to me once in a dream I had on three consecutive nights. The first night He said to me, 'What would it look like if there was no fear?' The second night He spoke the word 'metamorphosis', and the third night I heard the song from Mary Poppins, 'Let's go fly a kite, up where the air is bright'. I knew God was inviting me higher and to see things from a heavenly perspective.

Colossians 3:1-3 says, *'If then you have been raised with Christ, seek the things that are above, where Christ is, seated at the right hand of God. Set your minds on things that are above, not on things that are on the earth. For you have died, and your life is hidden with Christ in God.'*

Metamorphosis speaks of transformation as with a caterpillar into a butterfly and it spoke to me of a change of thinking and behaving. God has made us in His image to be like Him and He wants us to think and live from this place of our true identity.

Courage can look like a lot of things. For me I know God has spoken about stepping out more in the area of healing. Courage has begun to grow in my heart to believe for more than I have yet seen. I wonder what courage looks like for you? It might be just telling someone you are a Christian, it might be speaking to someone who inspires you, it might be forgiving someone, or it might be telling someone how you are really doing.

Courage doesn't mean we don't feel afraid; courage is actually stepping through fear and not allowing it to stop us. Instead of a feeling, it's a choice. It's choosing to lay aside our comforts, our fears of what others think, our fears of looking foolish, and our fear of failure, all because we know God has told us to go and that He will be with us. God said to Joshua, *'Be strong and of good courage, do not fear nor be afraid of them; for the LORD your God, He is the One who goes with you. He will not leave you or forsake you'* (Joshua 1:9 NKJV).

When the twelve returned from spying out the Promised Land they brought back fruit. They reported to Moses that it was a land flowing with milk and honey but that the occupants were like giants. Because of their fear of the giants, ten of the spies were afraid to go up but Joshua and Caleb had a different spirit and said, *'Let us go up at once and occupy it, for we are well able to overcome it'* (Numbers 13:30). They knew there were giants but their eyes were fixed on the promise and the prize; they saw what was possible and believed God was with them.

Throughout scripture we see God telling His people to trust Him and to be courageous. What always encourages me is that God uses weak people: people like Moses, Gideon, Rahab and Peter. Hudson Taylor said, 'All God's giants have been weak men who did great things for God because they reckoned on Him being with them.' In the same way, God wants to use you and me.

Our motivation for being courageous comes from simply believing that apart from God we can do nothing, but with God nothing is impossible!

CHAPTER EIGHT

The Costa Story

**So then, as we have opportunity,
let us do good to everyone.**

Galatians 6:10

In our current coffee-drinking culture where people head to cafés to either sit, to work or to connect with friends, a coffee shop seems an ideal place for us to show up and share the love of Jesus with people.

I had been sensing for a while God was speaking about some kind of café ministry and so when my friend Jules told me about a group of Christians near Bristol who were going into a Costa store and offering to pray with people, I was excited. This group had seen several people healed and one woman who had come in asking for prayer for forgiveness had then opened her heart to Jesus. Inspired by their stories I said to my friend I would love to see something similar in Bedford, and over the next few weeks we began to dream and pray about what that might look like.

We were still praying when one day I was sitting with another friend in our Costa store in Bedford and a conversation naturally opened up with the manager. As we were talking I felt the Holy Spirit prompting me to tell him the story of what was happening near Bristol and then to ask him what he would think of the same in Bedford. To my amazement he said, 'I would love that,' adding later, 'I would be excited for this to happen in my store.' We were massively encouraged by the manager's response and agreed to arrange a meeting sometime soon to discuss it further.

We were still praying about it when one morning I felt God say to me, 'You need to put legs on this!' It had somehow felt safe sitting in my bedroom talking to Jesus about the idea but, as with any pioneering endeavour, taking steps to see something become a reality always requires taking a risk, which is a bit scary. After talking it through with two of our church leaders, I arranged a follow-up meeting with Chris, the manager.

As we went into the meeting we were all agreed that we wanted to take time to honour Chris and his staff and not simply to come in with 'our agenda'. We also wanted to find out when would be suitable for them to have us come in and pray, and even where we might sit. We soon discovered that none of these details seemed to concern Chris because the very next thing he said to us was, 'You can come whenever you want, do whatever you want and sit wherever you want!' He even suggested the best place for our banners so that people would be able to see them properly! God was clearly giving us massive favour and opening a wide door to us.

As God continued to speak through prophetic words, words of encouragement and two dreams, I knew He was confirming that this was His plan. In one dream I was holding a newborn baby and trying to feed it solid food; as I offered the baby to a friend she commented that the baby looked like me. A baby in a dream can symbolically represent a new ministry. I took from this that God was saying this ministry looked like me and I was to lead it but not to rush ahead of Him. In the second dream I was trying to find a bus and was told there wouldn't be one until June. This was six months away and although we didn't feel we should delay starting, we wondered if in six months' time there would be some kind of acceleration. There was. Just six months after starting out we saw four healings on one afternoon!

Gathering a team

When pioneering anything in the Kingdom it's so important to have others go on the journey with you; courage buddies who stand alongside you and who remind you of what God has said when you are tempted to lose heart. Steve, who is an evangelist and one of our church leaders, has joined our team and continues to champion and encourage us on this journey. My friend Wendy has mentored and cheered me on hugely and there are many other friends who do too. After contacting the group in Bristol to ask questions about their café I was so encouraged by their story but was feeling a little overwhelmed by the details. I was very thankful when my friend Jules sent me a timely text saying, 'Step by step, my friend. He'll lead. He has a way and expression and unique doors for Bedford. Time to dream!' These words brought peace to my heart. I knew the way God had brought it all about was because it was His idea and I wanted to stay close. Hadn't He already spoken that to me recently when He'd said 'Walk close to me'? One of the lies I had believed at the start was that others would be excited about the idea but no one would join me and I'd be trying to do it on my own. I soon got to laugh at this lie as I saw the goodness of God to provide such an amazing team of friends as well as finances too. After our banners and flyers had been designed and printed[1] and we'd gathered a small team, we began one Friday afternoon in January of 2018.

We were all excited and nervous as we stepped through the doors of Costa, wondering what God might do. We'd picked our spot in the upstairs corner of the café where Chris had kindly cordoned off an area for us, and where we were hoping to cause as little disturbance as possible. I remember how putting up the two banners was our first act of courage and then, somewhat awkwardly, we stood around waiting to see what would happen next!

The first person we met was a young man who accidentally sat inside 'our area'. We were glad he had and one of our team went to speak to him. He'd recently been diagnosed with depression and was very open to receive prayer. After Hannah had prayed for him he told her, 'I think I am going to cry,' and

Hannah was able to share with him how much God loved him. Meanwhile, I had seen a young girl sitting with her boyfriend who kept looking at our banner and so I went over to chat to her. Explaining why we were there, I asked if there was anything she would like prayer for. She told me that she had twisted her hip and it was painful. Her boyfriend looked a bit uncomfortable but she was still very happy for me to pray for her. I laid my hands on her hip and prayed a short prayer commanding all the pain to go and for Jesus to heal her. She didn't want to get up and test it out there and then but later when they were about to go I asked her how it was. As she walked towards the door she walked up and down testing it out and then, with a big smile and looking surprised, she said there was no longer any pain. Her name was Champagne and she told us that her mum came to our church. On our first Friday we'd seen God touch two people: one physically and one emotionally. We'd been able to bless several homeless people with drinks outside the café and we'd met someone called Champagne. We had lots to celebrate!

We soon realised that if we were to get to pray for people who were on crutches or struggled to walk we needed to be on the ground floor, and so the following week we decided to position ourselves downstairs in the heart of the café. This was actually the area the manager had suggested to us at the outset and we've been there ever since.

How it works in practice

We occupy a couple of tables next to our banner and generally have two of our team at each table, available to chat to people. We move around, sometimes going outside the café and sometimes sitting at other tables and praying. We have had customers who have approached us but more often than not we are asking the Holy Spirit to highlight people to us. Sometimes what gets our attention is simply someone's openness to us: people of peace who smile and are drawn to us.

Gabrielle saw our banner and came over to say how much she liked what we were doing. We asked if she would like prayer for anything and she said for protection from infection in the lead up to an operation she was due to have. She also told us her relationship with her dad was difficult. We asked her if she knew Jesus and she said she did. She had a Catholic background. She spoke of having known God's closeness at times in her life. She was keen to ask about each of us, so we got to share testimony of Jesus in our lives before praying for her. We shared words of knowledge we felt God give us for her about knowing God as a perfect Father and Jesus as her older brother. Our words seemed to resonate and she began to well up. Good male role models, she said, had been lacking in her life. As we prayed for Gabrielle to encounter God's presence, she closed her eyes and afterwards told us how she had felt two arms coming towards her in an embrace and thought it was one of us offering to hug her. We knew this was God.

Sometimes we may see someone has a walking stick and is limping, or someone who looks lonely. When we sense God getting our attention we ask each other if God is saying anything to us about that person before we step out and approach them.

One time, two of our team spotted a young couple sitting at a table and between them felt God say a couple of things: that the girl was a poet and wrote poetry as a way of her expressing her emotions, and that she was afraid of putting herself out there. They had the phrase 'tall poppy syndrome' which is a fear of what you achieve being discounted or criticised. With encouragement from the others they approached the couple and asked the girl if she liked to write poetry. Looking slightly freaked out, she said, 'Yes, how do you know that about me? Who are you?' After explaining who they were and that God speaks, the girl, who was called Christine, told them she was both a poet and a playwright. When they shared the other word they'd had she really identified, in fact she told them she had been in a meeting earlier that day with a local theatre in Bedford to discuss about them potentially hosting her plays; she was waiting to hear back and was feeling quite vulnerable.

They then got chatting to her boyfriend. Ben was a musician who hadn't been able to fulfil his dream of going to music college due to severe tinnitus, which he'd had for eight years. The team offered to pray for his ears. Although he was sceptical, he agreed. As they were praying they could see by the look on his face that something was going on and asked him what was happening. He put his fingers in his ears and said he couldn't hear the ringing sound that previously had been constant. He said, 'It's gone!' Instead he was feeling a release of pressure and blood rushing into his ears, which he hadn't experienced for a long time. He looked completely shocked. As they spoke about how only knowing God can bring true joy and purpose, he told them his mum was a strong believer and prayed for him and 'though he wanted the switch to flick on inside of him, it hadn't happened yet'. Ben also told them when he was twelve he and his mum had been in a serious road accident and she had been told she'd never walk again. Now, he said, she runs up and down the stairs; he had clearly seen God answer her prayers. Using the 'Jesus at the door' illustration[2] they shared the gospel with Ben and asked if he wanted to open his heart to Jesus. Ben said he had lots to think about and wanted to go away and process it all. Through simply hearing the word 'poet' and stepping out in faith, my friends got to be part of a beautiful encounter only God could have set up.

There are many times we have stepped out with words that we felt God had given us. Sometimes, like this, they have been spot on, but there have been many times, too, when they haven't. We are ok with that because we know we are learning to hear God's voice. We know God loves to speak to us as His children and through us to show people His love. It's an exciting adventure learning to lean in and listen and we know God is training and discipling us as we go. When we step out with a word for someone we never want the focus to be on our gift but on God's desire to love someone. There have been some beautiful moments where we have been part of seeing God love someone this way.

Approaching people

There are no formulas, of course, but whenever we approach people we smile and want to be natural. This may seem obvious but if we're fearful and thinking about what we're going to say, it's easy to forget to smile and instead appear tense or awkward, which is intimidating for the person we're speaking to. We also want to be sensitive in recognising people's personal space and not be weird or freak people out. We might say something like, 'Hi, my name is Claire and I and my friends are in here today offering to pray for people. Is there anything you would like prayer for?' If we feel God has shown us something for them we might say, for example, 'I know this may seem a bit unusual but does this mean anything to you? I'm a Christian, I believe God speaks today and I felt God point you out to me. Can I share with you what I felt He showed me for you?' If people don't want us to share with them, we just smile and say thank you and wish them a very good day. There have been many times, though, when people have welcomed us sharing with them.

One time, three of our team felt God highlighting a couple in the corner of the café and Jess went and asked if they'd be open to our team sharing words from God for them. They were really open and asked all three to sit down at their table. The team had a sense that God wanted to speak about family and had three words of knowledge which were 'railway', 'gardening' and 'foreman'. Even though the words seemed very random they stepped out in faith and shared them with the couple. When Jules asked if the word railway meant anything to them, the lady, who was called Doris, said her great grandmother had died in the 1927 Darlington rail disaster. This had been tragic for her mother and then added her grandfather also had been killed on the railway. They then asked about the word 'gardening'. Doris welled up saying her father had lived with them until he had died recently and that he had loved gardening. Tim asked about the word 'foreman' and discovered their son was a foreman on a building site! Clearly God wanted them to know how intimately He loved them and knew them and all that had happened in their lives. Doris' husband James asked about their faith in God. He said he knew church was a place where people went to find strength but he was sceptical. They spoke with them about Jesus and Tim told the story of how God had healed him from curvature of the spine and asked if either of them had any pain or sickness. Doris said she had pain in her back and so they prayed for healing and that she'd know Jesus' love and comfort. After prayer she said she had no pain but would let them know if something changed after walking around. They talked about how Jesus had picked them both out because He loved them and there were lots of warm smiles and laughter before they went on their way. I know my friends came away amazed and delighted at how God had used them to share His heart.

Sharing the gospel

Signs and wonders help authenticate the gospel and, whether we have opportunity to share the full message of Jesus or not, we know that when we pray for the sick, God's Kingdom always comes near. Our aim is always to share something of who Jesus is and why He came for us and to point people to Him.

As a team we had felt drawn to two young girls at the next table to us. They smiled and were listening in to our conversation with the manager. One of the girls, called Julie, worked at another coffee shop and said she'd like to work in a store where the manager is as passionate about his staff as Chris is. After hearing about their jobs and dreams, my friend Tim asked if either of them had any sickness or pain. Julie shared that she suffered from mental health problems. She had been diagnosed with bipolar/personality disorder and had had it since her parents divorced when she was little. We listened and felt compassion for her and shared a story of someone who had encountered breakthrough in this area. Julie then let us pray for her. Tim asked if they knew about Jesus and they both said that they didn't. Tim shared the gospel with them, Jules shared the 'door' illustration, and I asked if they wanted to respond to Jesus knocking on the door of their hearts. They both said they did and we then had the joy of leading them in a prayer to receive Jesus and to be filled with the Holy Spirit. Afterwards they both said that they felt really happy and peaceful inside and we could see it too. We gave them Bibles and exchanged numbers so we could stay in touch. Julie stayed in touch for a while and said she wanted to come back and see us but after several texts she stopped connecting. Obviously we felt sad about that but we still choose to celebrate that we had the opportunity to tell two young girls about who Jesus is and lead them to Him. We know we can fully trust God for His care of them and that their future is part of a much bigger picture.

Documenting stories

We always want to be a people who tell stories of the goodness of God. From the start we have documented all we have seen Jesus do in the café and, to date, we have over four hundred stories. Some are about simple connections we've made with someone, a brief conversation, or opportunity to demonstrate His love over a cup of coffee. Many others are stories of bringing comfort, healing and words of knowledge. We record stories for two reasons. The first is that we always want to stay in a place of thankfulness and the second is that, through reading what God has done before, it raises our faith for what He will do again. Documenting stories also means when we forget people's names it gives us a way of tracking who we've met in case we meet them again.

Our cultural values

The journey God has taken us on has been amazing and we don't ever want to take it for granted. We count it a privilege that each week we get to meet people in our community and share the love of Jesus with them and that we get to sit with those who Jesus loves and died for. As a team we are seeking to establish a culture based on Kingdom values. Many of these are representative of our culture at King's Arms Church. We want to honour and model these both to one another and to the people we meet, and they have become our core values.

Generosity

We offer to buy a drink, whatever size, for every person we meet and give them as much time as they want to spend with us. We take opportunities to bless the people we meet. We have given gifts, birthday surprises, paid it forward for people in the queue, as well as blessing the staff. On a few occasions we have given different staff chocolates and a card filled with prophetic encouragements, which we have asked God for during the week. As a team we want to always model generosity to one another too. Jesus said, *'By this all people will know that you are my disciples, if you have love for one another'* (John 13:35).

Acceptance

However different people are to us we want to show them how loved they are as Jesus would. Heidi Baker says it so well, 'The Master created every precious soul who lives and no one is beyond redemption. Every living human is worth the effort of pouring out the radical love of Jesus.'

Courage

Courage can look like many different things. Sometimes for us it is just being in the café when only one person shows up. Sometimes it is stepping out with a vague impression to share a word of knowledge with someone, or it is sharing the gospel, or praying for someone to be healed. We are all growing in courage and cheer each other on as we see one another taking risks for the Kingdom.

Honour

Showing honour causes people to feel valued. We seek to honour the people we meet by respecting their personal space, being sensitive, gentle and always asking their permission before we pray or put our hand on their shoulder. If people change their mind and choose to leave we make sure they feel no pressure to stay and that they leave feeling loved. We honour the Costa staff who are generously sharing their premises with us and we look to support the Costa Foundation, which is their charity.[3]

Authenticity

Being authentic is powerful. It brings us closer together as a team, it breaks down unrealistic expectations and fear of being judged or making comparisons, and releases us to be all we are meant to be. We regularly tell each other how we are doing and pray for each other and remind each other of who God says we are. We have experienced weeks where we've been so encouraged and elated because of the miracles we have seen God do and we have also had weeks where it's felt tough and where we've had to encourage one another to keep going again!

Encouragement

We encourage those we meet, we encourage the Costa staff, and we encourage one another on the team. We each have different gifts and we encourage one another on the team to be fully who they are. Encouragement is powerful and, whatever sort of day someone is having, a word or act of encouragement can strengthen and empower someone to get up again and keep going. We love sharing words of encouragement with staff and people we meet and seeing their reactions and often their tears. One time we simply wrote a birthday card for a member of staff and he proudly displayed it on top of the coffee machine for all to see.

Thanksgiving

As a team we regularly share stories. We often share a story before we pray for someone. We share stories in the church, with each other and also when we travel on ministry trips. Sharing stories reminds us of what we have seen God do and keeps us being thankful. Whether we meet one person or many, whether we simply get to encourage, or whether we see someone healed or open their heart to Jesus, we celebrate God's goodness. At the end of our time in the café we always debrief, share stories and take a few moments to thank God together.

Training

As a team most of us have attended the training school at King's Arms Church in Bedford, which is called 'Training in Supernatural Ministry' (tsmbedford.org). This school runs annually from September to June and I highly recommend it. We are all still learning, of course, but this training has definitely equipped me and many others to live with a growing expectation to see more of God's Kingdom breaking out around us wherever we go.

Advertising

Our pull-up banners and flyers say, 'Do you need healing emotionally or physically? We'd love to pray for you' with a link to our church website. On the reverse of our flyer it reads, 'We believe in a God of love, who wants to demonstrate His kindness to us. So whether physical or emotional, whether times are great or challenging, we would be delighted to take the opportunity to pray with you or even simply offer a listening ear.' We also advertise who we are via our Facebook page. With social media being the platform through which many people communicate, it's a great way to let people know who we are. We try to keep it up to date with stories, photos and invitations of where people can come and find us. Why not check it out? You can find us on www.facebook.com/healingatcostacafebedford or by emailing info@kingsarms.co.uk.

Nearly two years into this adventure we have met so many different people, from many walks of life. As well as the friendship we are building with the Costa staff, we've met musicians, artists, students, business people, and those in the caring profession. We've met those who are poor and broken and those struggling with addictions, mental illness and loneliness. It is such a privilege sowing seeds of the gospel. Through prayers, acts of kindness, listening and offering acceptance and friendship we have seen many touched by God's love.

This Costa story is about the favour of God. I don't pretend to understand it; I just know it is God who opens doors for us to walk through, that He has called us to be pioneers and He is waiting to give us extraordinary favour if we are willing to step out and trust Him.

We are not all called to the same area of influence but we are all called to have Kingdom influence. If you're not sure where that is or what that looks like for you, why don't you ask God? I really do believe there are Kingdom stories God has already written for each one of us to be a part of.

CHAPTER NINE

Every Day, Everywhere

And proclaim as you go, saying,
'The kingdom of heaven is at hand.'

Matthew 10:7

Everywhere we go, we meet people: people who are just a step away from experiencing the Father's love.

I was in Leicester and a friend and I felt the Holy Spirit draw our attention to a lady sitting on a bench who was wearing a bright-pink coat. After introducing ourselves and asking how her day was going, the lady told us she was very tired because she was having problems sleeping, in fact she had been awake since two o'clock that morning. We felt compassion for her and as we listened, she became tearful and seemed overwhelmed that we'd stopped to talk to her. This lady, who was called Sally, began to open up and tell us her story.

Sally had loved her job helping children who had learning difficulties, but she was now no longer able to work because she was facing several big health issues. Feeling lonely and depressed she said she'd been wondering if God was there at all and had asked Him that very question a few nights before. Unable to sleep she'd said to God that if He was there, would He please give her a sign? She then hesitantly said to us, 'Maybe you are that sign!' We guessed that we were and we both felt His presence in that moment.

As we talked to Sally about Jesus she remembered that she had done an Alpha Course twenty years previously. She also remembered praying to receive Jesus into her heart but circumstances since had overtaken her. As we spoke about God's love and purpose for her she was tearful and we could see how our words were connecting with her heart. It was a precious moment as she responded to us inviting her to recommit her life to Jesus. There and then on the street we led her in a prayer, at the end of which she said, 'Whilst you were praying, I thought to myself, when I go home I'm going to give all my burdens over to God.' It was a wonderful moment of the prodigal Father calling His daughter home. We also prayed for God to heal Sally from digestive troubles that she suffered with and she said that as we prayed she had felt heat in her chest. After exchanging numbers and hugs we watched Sally go on her way, looking very different, and we went on our way wanting to sing and dance at the goodness and kindness of God who simply showed us to stop for a lady in a pink coat.

We are sent

In the gospels we see how Jesus met with people when He was passing through or on His way somewhere. He spoke with the woman at the well as He was passing through Samaria, and He met with Zacchaeus as He passed through Jericho. On His way to the Jewish feast in Jerusalem Jesus stopped for the man lying by the pool at Bethesda, and on His way to Jericho He stopped for the blind man who called out to Him. It was the same for the disciples too. Peter and John prayed with the lame man as they were on their way to the temple and, in Philippi, Paul and his friends met Lydia as they walked to the river looking for a place to pray. As the Spirit led Jesus and the disciples to meet people, so He wants to lead us in the same way.

Every day we are passing through on our way somewhere, whether that's to work, to the shops, to an appointment or even just out for a walk with the dog. Every day as we connect with people there are opportunities to share the love of Jesus and to demonstrate the Kingdom. I wonder in your everyday life do you carry an expectation to share God's love and to see signs and wonders as you pray for people? This is what I believe 'being sent' means: every day and everywhere we go!

Your 'every day' may be in your work place as you demonstrate Kingdom culture in the way you lead or in the way you work alongside others. As you represent Jesus be expectant of conversations the Holy Spirit might lead you into. You may be in a season of being a mum with lots of young children to care for and your 'every day' is amongst the mums you meet. The way you speak to and about your children, and the way you reach out to others, is how others will see Jesus in you. For some it may be amongst your neighbours, your family or your friends. Wherever your 'every day' is, be ready to love and to proclaim the gospel!

When Jesus told the disciples, *'As the Father has sent me, even so I am sending you'* (John 20:21) He was passing to them the same mission He had received from the Father. Promising His presence, power and authority, He told the disciples, *'These signs will accompany those who believe: in my name they will cast out demons; they will speak in new tongues; they will pick up serpents with their hands; and if they drink any deadly poison, it will not hurt them; they will lay their hands on the sick, and they will recover'* (Mark 16:17-18). We see in the gospels how the disciples didn't just receive this power and authority to bless each other but instead they went out to show and tell the good news of the Kingdom.

Every day, as Jesus walked through towns and villages, He stopped for the one. He reached out with love and forgiveness towards the woman caught in adultery and He heard the cry of blind Bartimaeus as He passed by, and stopped to heal him. On His way through Galilee Jesus delivered a man who was oppressed by demons and as He passed through Cana He healed the nobleman's son who was at the point of death. Jesus ignored those who tried to discourage Him from stopping.

Instead, He was listening to His Father and moved by the cry of people's hearts.

When the disciples returned and found Jesus talking to the woman at the well, not only were they surprised He was having a conversation with a woman, and a Samaritan woman at that, but also that He hadn't stopped for lunch. When Jesus told them, *'I have food to eat that you do not know about'* (John 4:32), they didn't understand, even thinking someone else had brought Him food. Jesus explained to them that His food was to do the will of the Father who had sent Him. He told them, *'Do you not say, "There are yet four months, then comes the harvest"? Look, I tell you, lift up your eyes, and see that the fields are white for harvest"'* (John 4:35). Just like the disciples and the seventy-two, Jesus sends us out into a huge harvest where we have the privilege of healing the sick, of bringing deliverance and of telling people God's Kingdom is right here on your doorstep.

Living a gospel lifestyle like this is not about us trying hard to bring Jesus into the conversation but more about us being Jesus in the conversation.

As we demonstrate the Kingdom it invites people to ask us, 'Who are you and why are you loving and not judging me?' 'Why are you being so generous to me?' And when we share words of knowledge with people and they ask, 'How do you know this about me?' we get to step aside and introduce them to the One who knows them by name. As we are intentional to go and love the lost, the Holy Spirit has all kinds of encounters like this for us to step into.

He knows my name

Jules was out with a friend and they were both looking for opportunities to love and bless people. As they stood in the town square they spotted a group of teenage girls hanging around. Sensing God wanted them to go across, Jules said to God, 'If you want me to go and speak to them, can you give me some kind of information about them that I couldn't possibly know, so it gets their attention and shows them you are real?' Immediately she heard the name 'Spencer' come into her mind. Thinking that sounded like a boy's name and that they were all girls, it felt random. They both took a deep breath and went over and introduced themselves and started chatting. After a while and having explained that they knew and loved Jesus, they asked the girls if any of them had sickness or pain in their bodies, which they could pray for. None of them did. They asked if there was anything else they would like prayer for but none of them were interested. When they refused, their hearts sank; they so wanted them to encounter God.

Suddenly, a fifth girl appeared and broke into the circle and said, 'Hey, what's going on? Who are you?' Jules and her friend explained and asked if there was anything she would like prayer for, saying that they believed Jesus wanted to bless her. She replied, 'I'm the last person God would want to bless.' They asked her why. She told them, 'I can't even say it out loud but if you knew the things I've done, you'd understand. Trust me, I'm the last person God would want to bless.' Jules told her, 'Jesus knows it all and He loves you, are you sure we can't pray for you about anything?' Again she said no.

It felt disappointing. Jules had felt sure God wanted to do something but it didn't seem to be going anywhere. As she asked the Holy Spirit what to say or do next, she suddenly remembered the name Spencer, which she'd felt God had spoken to her earlier. Jules asked if the name meant anything to her and immediately she could see it did as the girl looked shocked, took a step back and said, 'That's my surname!' This girl, who had no idea that Jesus is real and He speaks, and suddenly a stranger knew her surname! She said, 'Ok, I'm freaked out, what is going on? How do you know that?' It was a beautiful and powerful moment where the reality began to dawn on her that maybe Jesus was real, and knew her. Jules asked her, 'How does that make you feel?' She said, 'Special!' Jules and her friend then got to speak with her about her value to God encouraging her to ask Jesus to make Himself known to her. Her name was Grace!

What is beautiful about this story is that this girl described herself as the person God would least want to bless, yet God picked her out to show her His unconditional love. He is kind and merciful and no one is ever too far from His pursuit of them. This encounter was a significant moment in Grace's journey towards knowing Jesus and we trust one day soon she will know freedom from the shame she is carrying. She was the one God wanted to encounter in that moment. It was just a question of timing!

So how do we tune in and learn to recognise the Holy Spirit in our everyday life when we are out and about? There is no worship music playing in the background. Out in the marketplace our senses are often bombarded instead with physical need, with sickness and pain.

When we walk around our towns and cities, when we're in our work places or travelling somewhere, what if loving like Jesus is learning to wait to see and sense what the Father is doing? Where is He calling us to go and who is the Holy Spirit drawing our attention to? I believe this is how we get to join in with what God is doing.

Look for people of peace

People of peace, as one evangelist describes, are like low-lying fruit waiting to be picked. People of peace are recognisable because they are open and warm with us, and to our message. They may want to serve us or spend time with us. In our prayer café in Costa we noticed this with a staff member. Pete regularly came to clear our table so he could chat to us. He welcomed us, and what we were there for, and asked us to pray for him on several occasions. A person of peace isn't just someone who is kind and friendly but someone God has prepared ahead of time to receive the gospel through us.

In Luke 10:3-9 Jesus introduces the idea of people of peace. Before sending out the seventy-two, He tells them, *'Go your way; behold, I am sending you out as lambs in the midst of wolves. Carry no moneybag, no knapsack, no sandals, and greet no one on the road. Whatever house you enter, first say, "Peace be to this house!" And if a son of peace is there, your peace will rest upon him. But if not, it will return to you. And remain in the same house, eating and drinking what they provide, for the labourer deserves his wages. Do not go from house to house. Whenever you enter a town and they receive you, eat what is set before you. Heal the sick in it and say to them, "The Kingdom of God has come near to you."'* Everywhere we go there are people of peace and these are the people Jesus wants us to intentionally look out for. Over the years, for me, this has sometimes been a neighbour, a mum at my child's school or just someone I have met. Who are the people of peace around you, I wonder? Who have you noticed seems to be inviting you into their lives? As you pursue friendship and take time to get to know them, why not ask God how you can serve them and watch to see what the Father will do.

To find people of peace, we have to also be ready to face those who reject us. Jesus said, 'If they welcome you, they welcome me. If they reject you they reject me' (see Luke 10:16). Being unashamed of the gospel and experiencing what Jesus Himself experienced is challenging. I don't like being rejected, none of us do, but Jesus has promised He will always be with us. As we rest in His approval He will keep giving us courage.

In pursuing people of peace, of course, we must not reject those who are resistant. I'm sure we all know stories of people who have seemed utterly closed to the gospel, yet who have since turned and followed Jesus. God's love reaches out to everyone and we ourselves are examples of this, His unwavering love and mercy. Instead let us keep praying, knowing that God never gives up on anyone. Peter reminds us, *'The Lord is not slow to fulfil his promise as some count slowness, but is patient towards you, not wishing that any should perish, but that all should reach repentance'* (2 Peter 3:9).

The message of the Kingdom is simple but urgent

Jesus said, *'Take nothing for your journey, no staff, nor bag, nor bread, nor money; and do not have two tunics'* (Luke 9:3). The disciples didn't need any paraphernalia. Travelling light kept them dependent upon God. They didn't rely on methods or any five-step programmes. Their message was simple. They demonstrated the Kingdom with power and authority and called people to repent and believe. Jesus was saying don't let anything get in the way of this simple but urgent message.

I'm sure many of us have come across styles of evangelism that have put people off; those on street corners with placards shouting hell and damnation as well as those presenting a soft gospel message promising a trouble-free life. The gospel Jesus and His disciples preached was undiluted yet full of joy. When we communicate the gospel let it always be with love and respect yet without compromise; that we know what we believe and why we believe it.

I am truly celebrating the shift we are now starting to see where the church is beginning to step outside of the building. Where previously we have expected people to find their way to us, we are more intentionally going out to meet people where they are. This is the church being seen as the light of the world. We are now hearing more stories of churches offering prayer on the street and planting seeds of the gospel through acts of love and kindness. There are many stories in this book of this kind of servant evangelism. As we keep doing this let's always be ready to take the next step; to share the gospel and be unafraid of the challenge that it brings. As Jesus went about doing good and healing all those who were oppressed because God was with Him, so we too are sent and anointed to do the same. The gospel is the most joy-filled message of good news.

The following three stories hopefully describe something of this. They happened as I was just going about my day: waiting for a bus, having my ears tested and having treatment for a painful knee.

A cup of coffee

It was raining and as I stood at the bus stop, a lady was drawn to my takeaway coffee. I quickly discovered that Helen worked in a Costa store in a nearby town and we soon got chatting both about her job and about coffee. By the time the bus came I knew we would probably end up sitting together and I was listening to see what God might do. As Helen spoke about the charity which Costa supports, it led to us both talking about generosity and Helen saying how much she wanted to teach her daughter about being generous. I began to share with Helen the gospel, about it being the greatest act of generosity, and then how I had become a Christian. I hadn't planned any of this; one thing just led to another. I noticed that Helen seemed really struck by the fact I had not been born a Christian but had become a Christian and that was the moment when I realised a seed had been planted. Helen had now reached her stop and had to get off the bus, but before she did she asked my name and also if I would pop in to where she works. Something had got her attention and she wanted to know more!

More than a hearing appointment

I was having a hearing test and the lady doing the test confirmed I had a significant hearing loss in my right ear. She was sympathetic and I thanked her for her care. I then told her that whilst pursuing getting a hearing aid I would also keep getting prayer. She looked surprised as I told her of people I knew of who Jesus had healed of deafness. I felt the atmosphere in the room shift and, dropping her guard, she began to talk to me about her beliefs. She told me she had been praying for her family. She was a churchgoer and though she hadn't yet seen any miracles of healing I could see that the stories I shared with her had stirred a hunger in her.

In the changing room

I was in the changing room after having had some hydrotherapy for my knee. At the time there was just one other lady called Joan who was getting changed and I noticed she needed a crutch to walk with. I felt drawn to offer to pray for Joan but I was wrestling with the lie that because I too had a physical need I was not much of an example of the healing power of Jesus. Pushing through this lie, I decided to ask Joan what was going on for her and if the hydrotherapy was helping her. She told me that it wasn't really because she had a long-term back condition. Asking if she had ever had anyone pray for her she told me she had been to a 'healing place' that wasn't a church, and then added nonchalantly that her pain was just something she would have to live with. My belief is that Jesus wants to show people otherwise. As this conviction rose up in me I asked Joan if she would like me to pray for her. I told her I'm a Christian and believed that Jesus heals today and that I had seen people's backs healed by Him. At first Joan seemed embarrassed but then let me pray for her. After praying once she said her back seemed less stiff. I asked if I could pray again and this time after praying she said it was very much easier and seemed really surprised. I asked Joan what she made of that and if she knew about Jesus. She said she didn't go to church but believed there was a God. As I shared the gospel with Joan she said to me, 'It's definitely something to think about.' I left it there as I could see she had to go.

Every time we make much of Jesus we sow seeds of the gospel. We may not necessarily be the ones who get to see the fruit but, as we've already seen in previous stories, others come along and the seed is watered. This following story of a student from our training course is told in the TSM book *Momentum*:

My friend and I went for a walk in the park and wanted to stop for coffee. We usually stop at the park café, but for some reason we kept walking and ended up in the town centre. We passed a homeless lady and my friend felt prompted to offer to buy her a hot drink. When we asked the lady what she would like, she told us she was ok because someone was getting her a drink already. Wanting to bless her more, we offered to get her some food. We went into Costa and at the till there was a girl I knew from our course buying the homeless lady a drink. In that moment we realised that we were both buying something for the same lady. We felt excited that God had clearly picked her out for us to bless her. We felt such a sense of God's love for her, so when we went back with her food we asked if she needed prayer for anything. She told us that her knee had been injured, and showed it to us. It was three times the size of her healthy knee because of swelling, and she was in pain. After the first time of praying she said she felt heat on her knee. This raised our expectation, so we prayed again. The second time we prayed, we could visibly see the swelling go down and then disappear. It was so exciting. The lady was in shock and as she still had a bit of pain, we prayed a third time. After the third time of praying the lady got up and started jumping and hopping saying, 'Oh my goodness, it's gone, the pain has all gone!' God had fully healed her; all of the pain and swelling had gone! We got to pray God's love over this woman and hug her, and tell her more about Jesus and church. We walked away so grateful to God and just felt amazed at how much He loved this lady to pick her out of everyone in the town!

God is distributing seed all the time. Jesus said preach the gospel in season and out, which basically means, anytime, every day and everywhere we go! Living this way may not always be easy, comfortable or convenient, but God will move through us if we are available to Him and obedient. It may sometimes mean missing our lunch or our agenda being interrupted and usually it means pushing through some fear, too, but this is gospel living: it's what we are made for!

The woman at the well

In John chapter 4 we read a story where Jesus pushed through a cultural barrier. His approach seemed so natural yet everything about this conversation was far from natural. Unrelated men and women never engaged in conversation and for teachers and rabbis there was an even stricter code: they were expected to avoid eye contact all together! It wasn't only the gender issues either: Jews and Samaritans despised each other.

Jesus demonstrates humility by asking the woman for water. When she questions why, He tells her that if she knew who He was she would be the one asking Him for water, but she doesn't understand. She has no idea of either who He is or of her spiritual need. Jesus was crossing a massive cultural divide to bring her the message that, in Him, there is no division: neither Jew nor Greek, slave nor free, male nor female but, in Him, all are one.

It was midday, an unusual time for a woman to be drawing water alone and Jesus knew why. She had things to hide; she carried shame and was probably a social outcast because of her illicit relationships. Jesus knew all of this before He even spoke to her. He doesn't lecture her because He knows she doesn't need a lecture; she needs living water. He knew, too, that her spiritual need was the furthest thing from her mind yet because He was moved with compassion, no barrier would stop Him ministering to her. John Stott, the renowned theologian, says, 'Without any fuss or publicity, Jesus terminated the curse of the fall, reinvested woman with her partially lost nobility and reclaimed for his new kingdom community the original creation blessing of sexual equality.'[1]

I love this story for so many reasons. Firstly, it reminds me that we are to go where the enemy says we can't! Secondly, I love that Jesus knew what was in the woman's heart before He even spoke with her and that He knew He was the only one who could set her free. Thirdly, I love how she encountered such acceptance that she forgot she was a social outcast and ran to tell a whole town and, finally, I love that because of this news many came to meet Jesus for themselves and became believers. To me this story is a reminder that

we don't need to wait for opportune times to share the gospel because when the Holy Spirit leads us, it is always an opportune time.

Every day is a God appointment because now is the day of salvation.

Paul writes in Romans 10:14-15, *'How then will they call on him in whom they have not believed? And how are they to believe in him of whom they have never heard? And how are they to hear without someone preaching? And how are they to preach unless they are sent? As it is written, "How beautiful are the feet of those who preach the good news!"'* What if Jesus really is in the hospital, at the supermarket, in the café or at the bus stop? What if He is at the school gate or at your place of work and what if He has sent you and me to meet people there?

My friend Wendy often asks God for opportunities to love people and to see Him move through her and she recently told me this story.

I remember going for an MRI scan and seeing God's Kingdom come. I don't really like to be in enclosed spaces, so I was grateful for the distraction of being able to listen to the radio. Half way through the scan I started to wonder whether God might want to use this moment as an opportunity to bless the MRI receptionist. I had never thought like this before during medical tests, but felt provoked by friends who had chosen to use every opportunity to reveal God's kindness. As the machine whirred round me I began to ask God what He wanted to say to the receptionist. I had a vague picture in my mind of the top of her neck, which I could have easily dismissed, but I decided to take a risk and see if I'd heard right. Once the MRI had finished I went to find the receptionist. I told her I'd been praying for her during the scan and asked if I could share what I felt God showed me. She was happy to hear, so I asked her if she had a problem with the top of her neck. She told me she did and that she'd struggled with pain there for three years. With renewed confidence I told this lady I felt God had shown me her neck because He wanted to heal her. She was happy for me to pray, so I held her hand across the desk and commanded all the pain to go. After two very simple prayers the pain had completely gone from her neck! I got to talk to my new friend a bit about what she believed and church, and then we said goodbye. How amazing is Jesus?!

My friends David and Judy are a great example too. They regularly have stories to share of conversations that have led them to talk about Jesus, to pray for people or to invite strangers into their home. Judy recently told me the following story.

David and I intentionally look to start conversations with people wherever we are to see what God might do and this one started with a man called Reg about five years ago in a coffee shop. It simply started with a comment about a coat motif! Reg is an early retired professional with a wealth of life experience. He is an introvert but a man of great intellect and able to speak knowledgeably and at length on most subjects. In our conversations, which took place every two or three weeks, we would often drop in comments about God's love and His ways. Despite it feeling a bit clunky at times, Reg would listen to us and agree, even borrowing Bible commentaries from us to use when reading his Bible each night.

It was whilst making an annual visit to his son overseas four years later that, out of the blue, Reg's son needed emergency brain surgery. It was a very critical and risky procedure and he was naturally extremely anxious about the whole situation. When Reg returned home after what turned out to be a prolonged visit I saw him in the coffee shop where he told me about the whole incident. He said that he had some further news but he wanted to tell David and me together. As you can imagine we were intrigued and arranged a meet-up the following week. Reg told us that when his much-loved son was facing the surgery, he knew it would not be right to bargain with God for his son's life and so he did the only thing he could do. He said, 'I surrendered my life to God.' When David asked him if his life had changed, he said, 'Completely!' We were so happy. Wow! Praise God! What a privilege for us to have been a part of his journey to the Father. And, by the way, the surgery was a complete success!

David and Judy told me that as far as they know they are the only people this very private man has told about his experience. He is avidly reading books by N.T. Wright and looking up talks on YouTube as they continue their conversations at irregular intervals. They told me, 'Even when we sow clunky seeds in love, it seems God can do amazing things!'

Navigating mystery

When God invites us to step into His shoes and follow where He is leading there is sometimes mystery. As we seek to make the love of God known and step out in faith we inevitably encounter some disappointments along the way. For example, we don't yet see everyone we pray for healed or come to know Jesus.

I was waiting for some friends in a coffee shop when I overheard a conversation at the counter between a barista and a man who was cleaning the shop's windows. The barista had asked how he was doing and the window cleaner had replied saying he was not doing that great because he had bruised his ribs and they were very painful. Noticing that the barista hadn't stopped to hear the man's reply I felt compassion for him. The man went outside and as my friends hadn't arrived yet I knew I had a small window of opportunity to go out and speak to him. I sat for a few minutes plucking up courage and thinking what to say before deciding just to go for it.

I explained I had just overheard his conversation, that I was a Christian and knew Jesus loved him and would take away his pain. I then asked if he would like me to pray for him. He was adamant that he didn't believe in God but I told him that I knew God loved him very much despite him not believing in God. The man was reluctant at first but did let me pray for him. I asked him afterwards how his ribs felt and he said they felt the same. I was surprised and I offered to pray a second time. Again it seemed nothing had changed and somehow I didn't feel he was up for me offering to pray a third time. I told him again that God really did love him and as I went to walk away he said to me, 'Well, you tried!' It felt awkward and I did feel some disappointment. Of course, it is possible that he didn't want to admit God had touched him or that he was healed later. Whatever happened or didn't, it doesn't change what I know to be true about God: that He is good and that He heals today. I know God doesn't want us to give up loving and praying for people even when we don't see immediate results.

Another time after stepping out and praying for a man's foot that was in a cast and nothing appeared to change I wondered why. I know not to carry offence towards God but there was a restless question in my heart, which God was about to answer.

Later that day I was driving home and as I stopped at traffic lights I noticed that the road was unusually empty and I was surprised. It was mid-afternoon when all the children are usually coming out of school and yet the road seemed deserted as it would be in the early hours of the morning, and I wondered why. As I patiently waited without a car in sight I found myself thinking how easily I could have driven through the lights if it were not for me knowing to be obedient. That was when God spoke to me and said, 'I am teaching you obedience even when nothing is visible.' I realised God was answering my question about healing and was teaching me something new.

You see, God doesn't want us to get mechanical about praying for people. Every time we step out and trust God we are being obedient to all that He is and to all He has said but the outcome is always in His hands to do according to His will and His ways. This is why it's important we keep short accounts with our disappointment so that we don't carry offence towards God. God is mysteriously good all the time and, as we keep staying in a place of thankfulness, I believe we will see the greater things that He promised we would see. I long to see more people healed of cancer and long-term health conditions. I long for the deaf to hear and for people who are blind to see. Knowing His unchanging goodness and mercy follows us all our days spurs me to pray and not give up.

Ben Fitzgerald, director of 'Awakening Europe', is a man who met Jesus in an encounter that deeply changed him. Since that time Ben has lived passionately about one thing: showing the world Jesus in his everyday life. His deep conviction is that the nations of the earth will only be transformed as radical believers, living free, proclaim Jesus boldly. He says, 'The time for shining the light of Jesus is now! As the church we will never change history from our armchairs at home.' He tells the story of how he and some friends stopped a man in the street who was dancing to extremely sexual music. They simply stopped him to tell him about Jesus and how God loved him and knew him, nothing more. The man had been living a dark and very crazy life and was honest about that but to their amazement he had been crying to God for the past four days saying, 'God, if you're up there please help my life and give me a sign.' When Ben and his friends told him that God loved him he said, with tears in his eyes, 'I can't believe this, God hears me and answered me today — today is my birthday!'

Another story Ben tells is whilst driving along the road a Hindu man glanced at him and God told him, 'Turn around, that man's heart is open to Me.' Ben turned around and went back to introduce himself and told the man that Jesus had asked him to stop. The Hindu man was so shocked when he heard this and asked, 'What should I do now?' Ben encouraged him to read the Bible and invite Jesus into his life. The man assured Ben that he would do this and was stunned that God had heard his prayers and sent someone to him. Ben writes, 'This took two minutes out of my life but the message may have changed his whole life.' Ben's question was, 'Why aren't we all doing this?' And his challenge is, 'Let's be the generation that listens and does this.'[2]

I'm provoked to live this way; how about you? Let's be people who press in to know the Father and His ways and then go and make Him known. When we know the bigness of who God is inside of us and how much He loves people, we will expect the miraculous to happen. As Christ's love compels us, we will begin to take bigger risks because the love of God removes fear. This is becoming my growing experience. I know that when I spend time drawing near to God and meditating on His word and the truth of who He says He is, faith rises in me. It's the same when I spend time with men and women who believe that nothing is impossible with God, their love for God and their faith in Him becomes contagious to me. As we pursue knowing

God intimately and walk with the Holy Spirit, His supernatural power and presence will flow through us. Even when we see people going through painful circumstances we will carry an expectation for God to break in because we know and trust that He is loving, all-powerful and always good. Jesus taught us to pray with expectant faith. He said when you pray to the Father, pray like this. *'Your kingdom come, your will be done, on earth as it is in heaven'* (Matthew 6:10). He was saying release through your prayers the blueprint of heaven, show people My Kingdom and My ways.

Every day and everywhere we go we are His hands and feet on the earth revealing His heart and helping people to find their way back to Him. Let's go and tell people who our Father is and what He is really like. *'For God so loved the world, that he gave his only Son, that whoever believes in him should not perish but have eternal life'* (John 3:16).

CHAPTER TEN

Passing it On

One generation shall commend your works
to another, and shall declare your mighty acts.

Psalm 145:4

Caroline had been a sports woman but as the result of a failed hip operation she now had very limited mobility in one of her legs: sometimes it would just give way and she would fall over. She lived with constant pain and found it difficult to sleep at night but she was reluctant to take lots of pain relief and was a non-complainer. My friend Valerie lived next door and one day she told Caroline the story of our friend Lizzie who God had healed from cancer. Caroline who is not a Christian but believes in the spiritual world was intrigued by this story and, as a result, Valerie decided to ask Caroline if she would like a few of her friends to pray for her hip and she agreed.

We met Caroline in Valerie's home and after putting her at ease we gathered round her and began to pray. It all happened very quickly. In fact we were still praying for her when she told us that all the pain had gone and she felt increased mobility in her leg. She was amazed and surprised, as we were too! She told us that the only thing she wouldn't be able to do would be to run for a bus or run across the road. We said to her, 'Why don't you try?' and with that she went out of the front door and ran across the road. God had healed her! We heard weeks after from Valerie that not only did Caroline now have zero pain but she had even been able to do a sky dive; something she definitely couldn't have done before.

When we tell people stories about the goodness of God we are inviting them to see the reality of who God is and to worship Him. When King Darius saw that Daniel and his friends were completely unharmed after being thrown into the lion's den, he declared, *'For he is the living God, enduring forever; his Kingdom shall never be destroyed, and his dominion shall be to the end. He delivers and rescues; he works signs and wonders in heaven and on earth, he who has saved Daniel from the power of the lions'* (Daniel 6:26-27).

Telling stories of what God has done is so important because it reminds us, and others, of who God is and how great He is. It reminds us of what He has said and what He will do again.

I remember meeting Melanie on a Sunday morning as she came forward for prayer. Previously, after successful treatment, she had been given the all clear from breast cancer but now, sadly, it had returned. Melanie was someone who shone with hope and the love of Jesus and I felt privileged to pray with her for another healing miracle.

The next time I caught up with Melanie was at a two-day healing school in Kent. Despite her radiant smile I could see how the aggressive treatment she had been having had taken its toll and I discovered she was soon to undergo a big operation. I was struck by Melanie's faith and perseverance in coming to a healing school and pressing in with faith knowing He is the God who heals today. During the school, a healing testimony was shared of a lady whose cancer had literally dissolved and turned to a blob of jelly. When Melanie heard this story she reached out in faith believing to receive the same miracle for herself. Following the conference, a friend in fact prayed for Melanie that her breast cancer would, in the same way, dissolve and turn to jelly.

It was a year or more before I caught up with Melanie to hear the rest of her exciting journey. Following the two-day school

Melanie, believing that God was healing her, had a scan a few days later, the results of which showed that there was now no evidence of cancer! Despite this miraculous news her doctor advised she went ahead with the planned surgery as they could still feel the lump.

Melanie had to go to London for the operation and she and her husband booked into hospital accommodation that was about 25 minutes away. On the morning of the surgery, because Melanie's operation was going to take many hours, they encouraged her husband to go back to where they were staying and that they would call him when they had finished. He had just returned to his room when he received a call saying he could go back because his wife was out of surgery. He was shocked as the operation was meant to be twelve hours or more but they insisted she was out of surgery. After sewing her back up and giving her mild pain relief they had been able to discharge her.

It was some weeks later, after Melanie's oncologist managed to finally track down the surgeon, that they were able to find out exactly what had happened. The surgeon explained that when they had opened Melanie up there was simply an empty shell floating in a jelly-like substance.

The same miracle that Melanie had heard testimony of had now become her own. Melanie's story reminds me that when we reach out and refuse to let go, like the woman with the issue of blood, His power is released and we step into something wonderful that only Jesus can do.

Write down the stories

Some years ago someone encouraged me to record stories and I am so glad I did because I know I would never have remembered them otherwise. Being intentional to record them enables us to go back and to read and remember what God has done. I write down everything: prophetic words, dreams and stories of healings. These days I am often in situations when I travel on teams where I am sometimes asked to share a testimony. Having recorded them means I can quickly find them. Recently I was part of a team travelling to a church in France where we saw God heal nine people! Whilst we were there I also had the privilege of helping to film some of their stories.

Everywhere we go stories demonstrate the goodness and kindness of God and release faith that God will do again what He has done before. When Jesus fed the five thousand He was not just caring for the needs of His hungry followers but He was teaching His disciples that they, too, could pray and expect God's supernatural provision. I remember a time when we only seemed to hear of miracles happening in faraway places, like Africa or Brazil. Now, on a regular basis, we are seeing God do miracles right here on our doorstep. We are seeing more people getting saved, more people being healed and more people stepping into emotional and spiritual freedom. As we travel both here and abroad we get to joyfully share with others what the Lord has done. Our stories are everyone's stories!

Tell the next generation

Before the people of Israel entered the Promised Land Moses issued a warning to them, that they should not forget the Lord who had brought them out of Egypt and the land of slavery. As they prepare to cross over, Joshua tells them, *'Choose twelve men from among the people, one from each tribe, and tell them to take up twelve stones from the middle of the Jordan, from right where the priests were standing, and carry them over with you and put them down at the place where you stay tonight'* (Joshua 4:2-3 NIV). These stones were to be a reminder to the people of Israel forever and Joshua tells them this memorial will cause the children to ask, *'What do these stones mean?'* (v.6). Joshua was speaking about emerging generations who would ask and then be told the story of what God had done, how He had delivered His people out of slavery and brought them into the Promised Land foretelling what Jesus would one day do on our behalf. Telling their stories would have continually reminded them of what they had seen, heard and felt as they escaped. It would help them never to forget how God caused the water to part before them cutting them off from all their enemies.

Do you ever take time to look back and remember all God has done in your life? To see how far He has brought you?

Recently our Training in Supernatural Ministry School here at the King's Arms Church celebrated its tenth year. Students past and present attended a day to celebrate and a book filled with stories of all God had done over the ten years was published. As we spent time worshipping together I felt God reminding me of the twelve memorial stones in Joshua 4; how God didn't want us to forget what He had done in and through us and to pass on the stories to our children. Our stories really are like memorial stones that invite people to ask us questions. I felt provoked in that moment too that we shouldn't just look back but expect to step into more stories, more breakthrough and more adventures in God.

Always give thanks

Our journey of knowing God takes us through all kinds of seasons. Sometimes we will be on mountaintops where it feels as though we can almost reach out and touch God, where faith is easy and everything seems possible. Other times we can be in deserts or valleys where we feel discouraged, maybe struggling to see or feel any connection with God and waiting for breakthrough. I often have friends who I am praying for who are in tough seasons and I'm sure you do too. In times like these we need each other to pray for us and hold up our arms. When we are feeling tired, disappointed or frustrated we can either find ourselves asking where is God or sometimes take offence even questioning God's goodness. We all encounter battles at some time or another: battles of ill health, financial hardships, family breakdowns, grief and loss or battles in the workplace. Embracing and processing the pain of all that we are feeling is so important whilst at the same time seeking to stay in a place of thankfulness. I know this is easy to say and often harder to do, but this is our victory and the key to overcoming. In Philippians 4:6 we read, *'Do not be anxious about anything, but in everything by prayer and supplication **with thanksgiving** let your requests be made known to God.'* There is something liberating about thanking God in a time of anxiety because it reminds us that there is nothing that can happen to us that God is not in control of.

Why not make being thankful a daily pursuit and discipline in your life? I don't always succeed with this but when I lie in bed at night and find myself analysing my day or focusing on the things that I didn't do so well, I try to remember to stop and to thank God instead. I start thanking Him for everything that went well and that God gave to me that day including the bed I have to sleep in. When we practise thanksgiving, faith rises in us and in those around us. Thanksgiving shifts the atmosphere from expecting little to expecting much. When I focus on thanking God for who He is it increases my faith and reminds me of who He is and what He wants to do through me.

Things I have noticed that stifle thanksgiving are passivity and over familiarity. At King's Arms we are pursuing a culture of thanksgiving and celebration. When stories are shared we often stand and cheer and clap. We are celebrating the goodness of God as well as people's acts of obedience and courage. This is part of our worship to God. The danger is when we start to become over familiar with stories being told and we forget to be thankful and to celebrate another back or knee that's been healed. If we only wait for the big stories to celebrate we will miss what God is doing in the small, and He is the healer of all. As we steward well what God is doing amongst us, I believe we will see the greater things.

I am learning this with our prayer café at Costa. When we first started out we were regularly seeing God do miracles of healing and giving us words of knowledge for people. We were full of faith and wonder at what God might do next. There have also been times, though, where it has felt quite hard; where we have turned up each week and prayed big prayers but not seen anything really significant happen in people's lives. I believe God is teaching us faithfulness and patience in these seasons, to keep sowing seed. To help us with this we share stories at the start reminding each other of what we have seen God do and before we leave we always give thanks. God wants us to stay thankful and expectant for what we will see. Even as I write this, in the last few weeks several people have encountered God's presence powerfully and tangibly as we've prayed for them. One member of the staff, having heard and seen this, recently approached us to ask for prayer. After experiencing some immediate relief from his symptoms we also had the joy of sharing the gospel with him.

Run with those who inspire you to faith

In Proverbs 27:17 we read, *'Iron sharpens iron, and one man sharpens another.'* Just as one piece of iron left alone will become blunt unless another sharpens it, so it is the same with us. We need others around us who will remind us of who God says we are and of what He has called us to; people who are full of God and full of faith, inspiring us to keep going and not to give up. I know how much I need this. I am so grateful for people in my life; courage buddies who spur me on. Do you have people in your life who you can run with? People who will hold you accountable, who ask you good questions and who are honest because they genuinely care about you? Don't run alone; find running partners.

Hebrews 11 reminds us that we are surrounded by a great cloud of witnesses: men and women who have gone before us. When I read their stories, as well as testimonies of men and women from past generations, I am provoked to ask the question, am I living my short life here on earth 'all in for God'? Our race will look different from other people's but let's not allow anything to hinder us as we run towards the goal. Jesus is bringing many sons to glory.

Keep taking risks

The first time I experienced physical healing was forty years ago. In my work at a residential school for disabled children I was often bending and lifting. My back was under strain and finally it had given way. I was in pain and had to be off work for a few days and everyone around me knew the reason. The following Sunday I was at church and a visiting speaker got up and said God had told him to change his message. He apologised that he had never spoken on healing before, that he had very little experience of it but that he felt God had impressed on him to speak about it. At the end of his message he rather nervously invited anyone who would like prayer to go to a room at the back where he and anyone who felt God had given them faith for healing would pray. Looking back now, I can I see how this man took a big step of courage.

I went to the room at the back and a small group of people prayed for me. I don't think any of us in the room expected anything immediate to happen but I left there excited for what God might do. None of the people at the school were Christians and I wanted them to know God was real. Taking a risk, I decided to tell them as soon as I returned from church that I had been prayed for and God had healed me. It was a statement of faith; I didn't yet know if my back was healed or not. The amazing thing is I returned to work the following day and had no further pain. I must add here that I am not advocating naming and claiming or pretending something has happened when it hasn't but, on this occasion, as I told others it really did come to pass.

What I am so grateful for is that this man was obedient to God and took a risk. Through his act of dependence and faith I was not only healed but he passed on to me faith to believe God for a miracle as well.

Disciples who make disciples

Some years ago I attended the funeral of a lady who played a significant role in my life when I first became a Christian. Forty plus years ago she and her husband 'adopted' me into their family and loved me in such a way that it led me to ask, 'What do they have that I don't?' This lady and her husband had been missionaries in Dar es Salaam in Tanzania since the early 1950s and with their six children had experienced trials and challenges not unlike those we read of in the book of Acts. Close to death, storms, fires, many hardships, and often 'going without' yet praising and giving thanks to God. As I sat in the service being reminded of the simple gospel that this lady and her husband had displayed right to the end, I was moved to tears and provoked by the legacy she had left to her family, to me and to so many more who had encountered her example. Her family and friends described her as a prayer warrior, a strong woman like Deborah, a mother in Israel, and someone who had finished the race well.

I recently met a husband and wife who were in their late seventies. They were new believers who had been led to Jesus by a ninety-year-old couple in a care home. The wife, who had no Christian background, discovered her aunt had been praying for her for 50 years! Since coming to know Jesus this couple had moved into a deprived area and were living on an estate reaching out to their neighbours with the gospel. At a time where many people of their age might be slowing down, this couple were making up for lost time and passing on their story of meeting Jesus. This story reminds me that we should never give up praying for people or telling people about Him. As we do we are passing on the greatest legacy of all, which is Jesus!

I wonder if you have had a Christian heritage: parents and grandparents who loved and followed Jesus or even someone in your family who was praying for you. Perhaps, like me, you didn't but whatever has gone before, God can redeem. He can start a new heritage through us. When Paul was in prison and writing to Timothy he said, *'I am reminded of your sincere faith, a faith that dwelt first in your grandmother Lois and your mother Eunice and now, I am sure, dwells in you'* (2 Timothy 1:5). Lois and Eunice are not mentioned much in the Bible but these women were influential in raising a man of God, Timothy, who was Paul's most trusted companion and disciple. Like Lois and Eunice, as mothers or fathers we are given the same opportunity to raise sons and daughters, men and women who will point others to Jesus. As mothers and fathers in the Kingdom of God the deposit we leave in our children and our spiritual children can affect generations to come.

Before my husband and I started a family a man prophesied over us that we would have many children which, as I remember, caused a ripple of nervous laughter around the room. He went on to say that he didn't know how many we might have in our natural family but he believed God had many spiritual children for us and that we would see many birthed in the things of the Spirit. I know this has come to pass. Not only have we been blessed with a natural family of three amazing children and nine gorgeous grandchildren, but across the years we have had many come through our home who we have shared our lives with as well as those we have met as we've travelled on teams to other towns and nations.

Passing on to others

One Sunday morning in a time of response, Simon Holley, who leads our church, prayed with me and said, 'Claire, it's time to take others with you.' A girl called Hannah, who I vaguely knew, approached me that same morning saying, 'I want to learn from you.' Now I meet up with Hannah and it is such a privilege to champion and encourage her as she brings the Kingdom in her workplace. Hannah carries such compassion for people, especially those who are broken, and she regularly provokes me through her stories. One time she came out with a group of us into our town to share the love of Jesus with people. After a little while we lost sight of Hannah. When we caught up with her we discovered she had been buying a pair of shoes for a man she had met who was in need. Where perhaps I and maybe others might have gone to a cheap shop, we discovered Hannah had bought an expensive pair for him. The following Sunday the man came to church wearing his new shoes and, soon after, he recommitted his life to Jesus.

Nadine is a girl I had briefly known in my previous church but not that well. Some years later we reconnected at a conference and I quickly picked up that she was carrying the heart of an evangelist and was hungry to grow. She asked me to pray for her and we exchanged numbers to stay in touch. Nadine soon began sending me stories where she was stepping out in the supermarket or at her children's school and in her everyday life sharing the love of Jesus with people. I was so proud of her. Now, along with her husband Matt in the church that they lead, they are teaching others what it means to live a naturally supernatural lifestyle. They regularly take small teams out onto the streets of Leicester to share the love of Jesus. Nadine often sends me stories of prophetic encounters she and others have had as they have gone out to love people and demonstrate the Kingdom of God. Nadine is running in her lane ahead of me and I am so encouraged that in a small way I got to ignite her passion to share the gospel and pass on to her.

Every Christian has a testimony to pass on, like the woman at the well who told her friends to come and see and a whole town then came out to meet Jesus. She had no theological training or understanding of Christian doctrine; she was not even totally convinced about Jesus herself but she had been transformed by an encounter with the Living One. Many believed because of her testimony. They said, *'It is no longer because of what you said that we believe, for we have heard for ourselves and we know that this is indeed the Saviour of the world'* (John 4:42) .

Reaching nations

As I've mentioned I sometimes get to travel as part of a ministry team to other churches both in the UK and abroad. I count these opportunities as such a privilege as both my husband and I get to give away to others. It may be praying for someone who has responded in a time of ministry and seeing them encounter God's presence, it may be praying for healing or deliverance or sometimes just chatting over mealtimes or with families we stay with. Some years ago someone prophesied over me that God had called me to be a mother of continents and nations. How cool is that?

One time I was in India as part of a small team. My friend Wendy had been invited to minister at a few churches there. Before going, a prayer team had gathered to pray for us all and as a team we received many encouraging prophetic words about the trip. One very specific word I received was that I would meet a small boy carrying a marble who was going to do much for God's glory in India and that the Holy Spirit would lead me to pray for him and he would always remember it. It was quite a word! Whilst I was there I looked out for him both in the churches and when we went to the slums but I didn't see this boy.

It was towards the end of the trip when as part of a church camp Wendy had been asked to lead a session with the children; she was teaching them how to hear from God. One little boy stood out to me. Whilst the rest of the children were happily drawing their pictures of what they felt God had shown them, this little boy was screwing up his face straining to hear God's voice. One of our team sitting with him was patiently reassuring him; hearing from God clearly mattered to him and he was very happy when he felt God had shown him what to draw. As I watched this happening I felt God highlighting him and giving me faith to pray for him. As I went to him I felt God say he was going to be someone like Samuel who would hear God easily. This boy wasn't carrying a marble and I don't know if he was the boy in the prophecy but I knew God was showing him to me. When I prayed and told him that I believed he would hear God's voice he seemed very moved and, pointing to himself, said, 'What, me?' Later I spoke to his mum to tell her what I had prayed. She said that she already had a sense there was something special about him and she went on to tell me two remarkable supernatural stories that had already happened in his life.

During our time in India we saw many people healed and set free. On one day we saw three people healed, two of whom had long-term health conditions. I saw one girl give her life to Jesus and another receive the baptism of the Holy Spirit and the gift of tongues.

Another time my husband and I were part of a ministry team visiting a church in Oklahoma. Some months previously someone had given us a prophetic word that on one of the trips we'd go on we would meet a couple who we'd deeply connect and stay in touch with, even visiting back and forth. We wrote it down and trusted God that on one of our trips we might see this happen but we never imagined it would be so soon. Todd and Kelli hosted us for the first two weeks of our trip and within a short time of staying with them we soon recognised that this was the couple! A few days in, Kelli told us how impacted she had been by our visit and all that we had shared with them. She showed us in her journal too where she had written, 'Please send someone to help us.' Even though to us we had just been sharing stories and sharing our lives, clearly we, along with the rest of the team, had passed on something significant that they needed at that time. As a result of attending the two-month ministry school, which Wendy and our team had gone to lead, we quickly saw this couple stepping into greater freedom and becoming the people God had called them to be. Wendy and I have visited Oklahoma since and Kelli has travelled to the UK on a couple of occasions as well as staying in touch via Skype. She now teaches and leads others in prophetic ministry in the church and has also started to take others out with her to share the gospel.

I still remember when Kelli stepped out with her first word of knowledge on a Sunday and God healed a man with a forty-year back condition. I also remember when she stepped out with her first word of knowledge outside the church and spoke to a young girl in the waiting area of a doctor's surgery. I got to stand alongside her and encourage and cheer her on for her step of courage and obedience.

Leaving a legacy

Championing others is how we actively pass on our inheritance. As in a relay race, we come behind, run together and then pass on the baton to those coming after us. The story of Elijah and Elisha stands out to me as one of the greatest examples of this. When it is time for God to take Elijah home, Elisha doesn't want to leave his side. It is Elijah who has been his spiritual father and mentor. Elijah then asks Elisha an important question. He says, *'Ask what I shall do for you, before I am taken from you'* (2 Kings 2:9). As a spiritual father he is being intentional about passing on a spiritual inheritance to Elisha. He knows that all God has given him isn't just for him but for the generations that will follow. Elisha replies, *'Please let there be a double portion of your spirit on me.'* As Elijah is taken up into heaven and Elisha sees him go he cries out, *'My father, my father!'* (v.12). I don't know about you but when I read those words I imagine the deep sadness he must have been feeling in that moment and how, because of disappointment, he could so easily have stayed in a place of self-pity and left Elijah's cloak on the ground. Instead he picks up Elijah's cloak, strikes the water of the Jordan in the way he had seen Elijah do, and crosses over. He received a double portion of Elijah's inheritance and we read the exciting stories of all that happened next in the book of 2 Kings.

This story is poignant for me. Some years ago God spoke to me in a dream and asked a question. He said to me, 'If the Lord took your Elijah away, what would you do?' At the time I knew God was bringing me a challenge. I was so inspired by the stories and examples of others who were living this way but often because of an orphan heart I doubted and compared myself with them. God was showing me that I, too, had an inheritance to live out and pass on to others. I know that God has called me to be an evangelist and to pursue living a naturally supernatural life every day, and this is my inheritance that I want to pass on to others. Jesus has often drawn my attention to Paul's word to Timothy. *'Preach the word; be ready in season and out of season . . . As for you, always be sober-minded, endure suffering, do the work of an evangelist, fulfil your ministry'* (2 Timothy 4:2,5). Paul's commissioning word to Timothy was as a father to a spiritual son reminding him of his purpose. Because I know Jesus has called me to introduce people to Him and to pray for the sick, these verses have been a great encouragement to me to keep persevering, especially in tough seasons. As God has reminded me of my purpose it has led me to act from a place of both intimacy and identity.

In Paul Manwaring's book *What on Earth is Glory?* he writes, 'We mustn't waste our victories. Each of them has given us a key to access heaven and bring it to earth in our lives and in the lives of others. Wise stewards don't simply walk around with the keys, wherever they have access they are about their master's business.'[1]

There is a real danger that we can go from Sunday to Sunday, read books, attend conferences and gather more and more information about God – without actually going and doing the works Jesus taught and commissioned us to do. We do actually have to GO!

We are living in exciting days and a time of advancement. We are seeing and hearing of more miracles and demonstrations of God's love and power in the lives of people who don't yet know him. There are more churches now regularly going into their towns offering prayer for healing, more ministry schools emerging equipping Christians to learn to live like Jesus and to do the things He told us to do. As Jesus is building His church God is raising up a radical supernatural army of followers of Jesus; ordinary people like you and me. As God is bringing a shift in how we see evangelism, He is reawakening us to understand our heavenly assignment: to go and preach the gospel and demonstrate the Kingdom as we heal the sick, cast out demons and even raise the dead! This I believe is the normal Christian life. In this book you'll have read many stories of God's kindness, of miracles and breakthrough, and of the courage of ordinary people who have simply stopped to love the person in front of them.

As others have gone before us, this is now our time and our assignment on the earth. God is passionate to demonstrate His Kingdom through you and me. As you ask Him in your 'everyday' where you can be His hands and feet, He will show you. His Spirit rests upon you and His power is made perfect in your weakness. Let's take every opportunity to make Him known. Let's go! Let's rediscover the joy of the great commission because this is what we're made for.

End Notes

Chapter 1

1. 'Out of Hiding' written by Amanda Cook and Steffany Gretzzinger (copyright © 2014 Bethel Music Publishing, administered by Song Solutions).

2. Larry Norman (1947–2008), an American musician, singer, songwriter, record label owner and record producer, was considered to be one of the pioneers of Christian rock music. He released more than 100 albums.

3. Randy Stonehill is an American singer and songwriter from California, best known as one of the pioneers of contemporary Christian music.

4. The Jesus Movement was an Evangelical Christian movement beginning on the west coast of the United States in the late 1960s and early 1970s, spreading primarily throughout North America, Europe and Central America before subsiding by the late 1980s.

5. The Four Spiritual Laws is an evangelistic Christian tract created in 1952 by Bill Bright, founder of Campus Crusade for Christ. Also used by the Navigator Ministry, Campus Crusade for Christ claims to have distributed 2.5 billion copies.

6. *The Living Bible* is a paraphrase of the Bible by Kenneth N. Taylor, first published by Tyndale House Publishers in 1971.

7. *Daily Bread* is a Bible reading guide published by Scripture Union.

8. 'Just as I am, without one plea, but that Thy blood was shed for me, and that Thou bid'st me come to Thee, O Lamb of God, I come, I come' is a verse from a poem written by Charlotte Elliot in 1835. Published in more than 1600 hymnals and reaching billions around the world, it continues to bring people to Christ even today.

9. The Parable of the Prodigal Son is one of the parables of Jesus in the Bible (Luke 15:11-32).

10. Phil Keaggy is an American acoustic and electric guitarist and vocalist who has released more than 50 albums and contributed to many more recordings in both the contemporary Christian music and mainstream markets.

11. Malcolm and Alwyn were a popular British gospel group in the 1970s. They played rock music influenced by Simon and Garfunkel, Bob Dylan and The Beatles, with lyrics reflecting their conversion to Christianity.

12. Keith Green (1953-1982) was an American contemporary Christian musician, pianist, singer and songwriter. Beyond his music, he was best known for his strong devotion to Christian evangelism and challenging others to the same.

13. The Quakers are a group of Christians who use no scripture and believe in great simplicity in daily life and in worship. Their services consist mainly of silent meditation.

14. Youth with a Mission (YWAM) is a Christian missionary and outreach group. Founded in 1960, the group's initial focus was to get youth involved in missions. Today, while maintaining its original youth-oriented ethos, the group has expanded its membership to those of older ages as well.

15. *Toymaker & Son* is a choreographed dance drama written by Colin Harbinson. The epic account of the most powerful rebellion in history, the greatest love story in the universe, and the most daring rescue plan ever conceived.

16. Church of the Nations is a family of churches that started in Crawley in the early 1980s. There are now churches in the UK, South Africa and America.

Chapter 2

1. The Alpha Course is a ten-week course that creates a space where people can bring their friends for a conversation about faith, life and God.

2. Training in Supernatural Ministry (TSM) based at King's Arms Church in Bedford is a nine-month training course designed to equip believers to live a naturally supernatural life. For more details got to: www.kingsarms.org/tsm

Chapter 3

1. Bob Johnson, *Love Stains* (Redding, CA: Red Arrow Media, 2012), p.158.

2. 'This Little Light of Mine' is a gospel song written for children in the 1920s by Harry Dixon Loes.

3. Sir Anthony Hopkins, from an interview with *Catholic Herald* in 2011. Used by permission of *Catholic Herald*.

4. King's Arms Church is where my husband and I now call home since moving to Bedford five years ago. For more information visit www.kingsarms.org

Chapter 4

1. *Finger of God* and *Furious Love* are two of a series of movies produced by Darren Wilson's Wanderlust Productions.

2. Heidi Baker, missionary, itinerant speaker, and the CEO of Iris Global, a Christian interdenominational, missionary organisation that provides humanitarian aid in Africa, the Americas, Asia, Europe, and the Middle East. Members of Iris seek to spread the gospel while performing humanitarian activities.

3. Father Heart Conference – where people can learn more about who God is as their Father and who they are as His sons and daughters. For more information on Father Heart Conferences run by King's Arms Church Bedford see: www.kingsarms.org/events

4. Bill Johnson, Sunday morning sermon 'Hear God's Voice', April 3rd 2019. Bill Johnson is Senior Leader of Bethel Church. For more information visit www.bethelredding.com

5. *Scattered Servants,* copyright © 2018 by Alan Scott. Used by permission of David C. Cook. May not be further reproduced. All rights reserved.

Chapter 5

1. Paul Manwaring, *What on Earth is Glory?* (Destiny Image Publishers, 2011), p. 123-124. Used by permission of Paul Manwaring.

2. Heidi Baker, 'Come Closer' from *Reckless Love* (Chosen Books, 2014), p. 42. Used by permission of Baker Publishing.

3. Ed Stetzer, 'Loving the Lost' blog, 12th January 2015.

Chapter 6

1. The King's Arms Night Shelter is part of the King's Arms Project: a ministry of King's Arms Church. It is a Christian registered charity set up to work with the homeless in Bedford. For more information, see their website: www.kingsarmsproject.org

2. *Piercing the Darkness* is a novel by Frank Peretti, first published by Crossway Books in 1989.

3. Bill Johnson sermon at Bethel Church Redding CA, 2nd June 2017.

4. Bob Johnson, *Love Stains* (Redding, CA: Red Arrow Media, 2012), p. 631–632.

Chapter 7

1. Jackie Pullinger, a missionary to Hong Kong since 1966 and author of *Chasing the Dragon*, first published by Hodder & Stoughton in 1980.

2. Brother Yun, an exiled Chinese Christian house church leader and evangelist, and author of *The Heavenly Man*, first published by Monarch Books in 2002.

3. Tracy Evans is a physician assistant and the founding director of iReachAfrica and Africa 180, which are committed to evangelism and reversing the cycles of poverty, disease and death in Mozambique. Tracy is also the author of *Outrageous Courage* published by Chosen Books.

Chapter 8

1. Our banners and flyers were designed by www.wewillrun. co.uk

2. 'Jesus at the door' is an evangelism tool. Founder: Scott McNamara an evangelist based at Causeway Coast Vineyard Church, Coleraine, Northern Ireland.

3. The Costa Foundation is an independent charity that aims to relieve poverty in coffee-growing communities. Its mission is to improve the life chances of children by providing them with the opportunity for a quality education.

Chapter 9

1. John Stott, *Issues Facing Christians 4th Edition* (Zondervan, 2011).

2. Ben Fitzgerald: two stories. (Unsure of source at time of writing.)

Chapter 10

1. Paul Manwaring, *What on Earth is Glory?* (Destiny Image Publishers, 2011), p. 154. Used by permission of Paul Manwaring.

Further suggested reading

Naturally Supernatural: The Normal Christian Life by Wendy Mann

Called to Influence by Karen Kircher

Multiplying Disciples by Phil Wilthew

Stepping into the Impossible by Mark Marx

Children and the Supernatural by Jennifer Toledo